Turning Notes into Music

An Introduction to Musical Interpretation

Hans Lampl

The Scarecrow Press, Inc.
Lanham, Md., & London
1996

SCARECROW PRESS, INC.

Published in the United States of America
by Scarecrow Press, Inc.
4720 Boston Way
Lanham, Maryland 20706

4 Pleydell Gardens, Folkestone
Kent CT20 2DN, England

British Cataloguing-in-Publication Information Available

Library of Congress Cataloging-in-Publication Data

Lampl, Hans, 1919–
Turning notes into music : an introduction to musical interpretation / by Hans Lampl.
 p. cm.
Includes bibliographical references (p.   ) and index.
1. Music—Interpretation (Phrasing, dynamics, etc.) I. Title.
MT75.L32 1996 781.46—dc20 96-7833 CIP MN

ISBN 0-8108-3164-3 (cloth : alk.paper)
ISBN 0-8108-3165-1 (pbk. : alk.paper)

To the memory of
Alice Ehlers and Muriel Kerr
who in their very different ways
inspired their students to mind the score

CONTENTS

Inadequacies of notation: "fixed" elements and variables—Some common
misconceptions: obstacles to the effective study of interpretation—The interpretive
process: the "area of appropriateness" and "individual choice"—Dealing with the
complexities of interpretation—Teaching musical interpretation—Accuracy and
"musical" performance—A book on musical interpretation: benefits and limitations
—Benefits of the Socratic method: engaging the student's mind—Individual chapters'
inventories of common interpretive problems—Active listening crucial to effective
performance—Examples of common pitfalls: performing without an adequate
"blueprint"—"Mishearing" by the listener and how to avoid it.

The term "dynamics"—Interpreting dynamic marks—Dynamics in contrapuntal
music—"Not seeing the forest for the trees"—Vertical balances—Melodic direction
and dynamics.

Fundamentals of performance—Dynamic inflections without dynamic markings—
Musical idea defined by disposition of accents—Function of the barline in fixing basic
accents—Some group accents more prominent than others: the *Grosstakt*—Focal
points—Dynamic implications of durational values—Meter not always in agreement
with barring scheme.

Finding and maintaining the "Right" tempo—Using the metronome—Tempo
markings—Clues in the score—Factors affecting tempo perception—Acceleration and
retardation—*Rubato*—"Rhythmic elasticity"—Function of *rubato* in defining
structure—Fermatas and other pauses.

The term "articulation"—*Legato*—The many degrees of separation—Interpreting slurs—Groups formed through articulation—Varieties of articulation—Attack and release—Shapes of longer notes—Syncopation.

PREFACE

One of the most fascinating aspects of musical performance is that a single piece of music can be interpreted in many different ways. It is equally intriguing that the performances of one and the same piece by different artists are all likely to be valid and effective, even though they may vary enormously. Some listeners will prefer certain versions to others; but different artists of equal stature always seem to receive equally favorable responses from their respective audiences.

How do these artists manage to sound so different and yet, each in his[1] own way, do justice to the music? This contradiction is only one of many aspects of interpretation which appear to defy definition. In fact, musical interpretation is often regarded as something of a mystery to be revealed, if at all, only at advanced stages of training. In reality, however, interpretation is an integral part of all musical performance, beginning with the most elementary level.

Before looking for rational solutions to the puzzles of interpretation, we should take note of certain facts:

1. All elements of music—such as melody, rhythm, harmony, and formal structures of all kinds—have their interpretive implications which in performance manifest themselves in varying degrees and inflections of tempo, dynamics, articulation, etc.

2. Except for the notes themselves—and the pitches and basic time values they indicate—these "elements of performance" are not fixed and are subject to modification by the performer, to "interpretation."

3. All marks of expression (p, ⟍, *sf,* etc.) and verbal directions (*andante, ritenuto, espressivo*, etc.) represent only approximate values, and the many nuances, which are an essential part of any "musical" performance, are only implied but not specifically spelled out in the score.

4. Taste and temperament, intuition and inspiration all play a role in musical interpretation.

Quite obviously, the elements in the last item are beyond our powers to quantify, let alone, to manipulate. Items 2 and 3 only seem to confirm the impression that specifics of interpretation (e.g., the exact tempo, the decibel level of a note, or the true length of a *staccato* note) simply can not be pinned down with any degree of certainty.

Nevertheless, the score itself provides the performer with all the clues necessary to enable him to determine the interpretive details of his performance.

The title *Turning Notes into Music* describes in a nutshell what this book aims to accomplish: 1. to identify the phenomena of interpretation which can indeed be identified, and 2. to chart

---

[1]The masculine pronoun is used throughout this book in a gender-neutral sense.

the steps which transform a literal rendition (merely "playing the notes") into a "musical"[2] and convincing performance.

The bulk of the volume is essentially a comprehensive annotated and illustrated catalog of interpretive problems the performer will have to recognize and address in the course of preparing a piece of music for performance. The material is arranged in separate chapters, each devoted to a single area of interpretation (dynamics, tempo, etc.) in order to allow for a clear focus and to facilitate comprehension.

As an introduction to musical interpretation the book does not attempt to deal with its most advanced and sophisticated aspects, let alone, ultimates of artistry. Neither does it set rules which would tend to inhibit the performer—to wrap him into an interpretive straightjacket, so to speak—nor does it point out "authoritative" performances to be merely imitated. But it does enable the aspiring performer to achieve a thorough grasp of fundamentals on which to build the concepts—his interpretive "blueprint"—for performances which satisfy the interpretive requirements of the music while allowing him to follow his artistic impulse. The performer who has learned to analyze the score with a view toward assessing these interpretive requirements will invariably be able to come up with the appropriate nuances and inflections, avoiding mechanical and "literal" renditions on one hand, and exaggerations and distortions on the other.

It should be understood, of course, that any analysis and consideration of details must be taken care of during the initial, preparatory phase preceding the performance stage. During the actual performance, any preoccupation with details is disruptive, interfering with the pattern of reflex actions into which all the elements of execution, of technique and interpretation, have been amalgamated in the course of preparation.

The many texts and "methods" available which deal with performance mainly address its technical aspects, with little space, if any, given to interpretation. When courses in interpretation are offered, they are most often limited to the performance practices of earlier periods. As a consequence many individuals preparing for teaching careers in the various areas of performance, including aspiring conductors, complete their formal schooling without being exposed to a systematic approach to musical interpretation. In the course of their training they will have listened to a considerable amount of music, played or sung in various ensembles, and studied voice or an instrument for a number of years, yet without ever developing meaningful and reliable concepts concerning the interpretive aspects of their own performance. In turn their students learn to rely mainly on imitation—of their own teachers' demonstration or the performances of established artists—rather than acquiring a secure interpretive grasp of the music they perform, based on thorough study and analysis of the score itself. *Turning Notes into Music* is intended to narrow the existing gap in the literature and pedagogy of performance.

Since musicianship and interpretive skills determine the quality of all musical performance—instrumental and vocal, solo and ensemble—this book is designed to cut across the entire panorama of performance. The basic principles of musicianship and interpretive requirements in general are the same for players of strings, woodwinds, brass, percussion and

---

[2]See footnote on p. 1.

keyboard instruments, and singers as well. This becomes particularly obvious every time performers join in ensemble, whether as soloists accompanied by one or more instruments, in chamber music, or in an orchestra or chorus. In spite of the enormous differences in quality and application the concepts governing interpretation are essentially the same for all of them. These concepts should always be the starting point for any consideration of technical procedures and adjustments in dealing with the idiosyncrasies of diverse instruments and the voice.

Turning Notes into Music represents a response to problems encountered and questions heard time and again over the years. Every statement reflects some actual occurrence in a long career of active involvement in many areas of musical pedagogy and performance. The book is relatively short; but most of the statements have wide ramifications, and text and musical examples together provide an ample framework for dealing successfully with a broad spectrum of interpretive problems. It is designed to serve a variety of purposes:

1. As a text for classes in musical interpretation;

2. As a guide for performers training to be teachers;

3. For collateral reading and study in performance-related classes, such as conducting, performance practices, instrumental and vocal literature and pedagogy;

4. As a reference tool for individual and class instruction in vocal and instrumental performance and conducting;

5. As a teacher's guide as well as for assigned reading and study under the teacher's guidance for students from an intermediate level and junior high school age on;

6. As resource material for amateur musicians and adult students of performance.

There are no prerequisites for the use of this book except a knowledge of musical notation and terminology and some elementary theory.

The chief value of this book is believed to lie in the description of phenomena of performance which commonly are left vague and undefined. Words alone, however, cannot pinpoint all subtle inflections of tempo, dynamics, articulation, etc. Since one audio example is "worth a thousand words," most musical examples have been recorded.[3] The tape serves several purposes:

1. To provide sounds to go with the score excerpts;

---

[3]Requests for the tape should be addressed to Hans Lampl, 610 Deer Pass Dr., Sedona, AZ 86351.

2. In some cases to offer illustrations of satisfactory and "musical" performances as well as questionable ones not arising from the context, i.e., the objective evidence in the score;

3. To stimulate the reader's perception and to help bolster his judgment by increasing his awareness of the wide range of options in all matters of interpretation.

When the printed score excerpt alone seemed to make its point, it was not recorded. In a number of cases the example in the text shows only one line or a small segment pinpointing the problem under discussion. The audio version, however, may be longer and more complete in order to provide a better sense of the musical context. In the choice of musical examples the main consideration was easy accessibility.

H. L.

ACKNOWLEDGMENTS

First, I would like to express my appreciation to David Kuehn, my Department Chairman at California State University, Long Beach, who allowed me to teach a course in musical interpretation. It was the participants in these classes who proposed that I write a text. Without them and the encouragement and support of my wife, Lili, I would never have settled down to the task.

Among the friends and colleagues who were interested in the project, read portions of the manuscript in its various stages and offered invaluable comment and criticism were Charles Aurand, Kristine Forney, James (Bud) Gould, Douglas Gallez, Royal Stanton, and James Decker. I cannot thank them enough.

I am particularly grateful to my daughter, Dodi Palmer, who produced the text on the computer, and to Lew Warde, who did an admirable job with the musical illustrations, using the *Finale* program.

Lili, who did not live to see this book completed, was most helpful in several ways: typing the first drafts and monitoring my progress throughout with her sound instinct for the proper turn of a phrase and her unfailing good judgment in musical matters.

Special thanks also must go to Don Hixon, librarian, author, and editor, for his positive response and assistance in the earlier stages of the project.

I would like to extend my gratitude to several publishers for granting permission to include a number of music examples and text passages, as indicated below.

Loewe's "The Heather on the Hill" from *Brigadoon*, music by Frederick Loewe, lyric by Alan Jay Lerner, ©1947 (renewed 1975) by Alan Jay Lerner and Frederick Loewe, world rights assigned to EMI U Catalog Inc. (Publishing) and Warner Bros. Publications Inc. (Print), all rights reserved, used with permission.

Erich Leinsdorf's *The Composer's Advocate*, ©1981, reproduced by permission of Yale University Press.

El Salón México (Aaron Copland) © Copyright 1939 by The Aaron Copland Fund for Music, Inc.; Copyright Renewed. Reprinted by permission of Boosey & Hawkes, Inc., Sole Licensee.

Kurt Blaukopf's *Gustav Mahler*, translated by Inge Goodwin (Allen Lane, 1973), copyright Verlag Fritz Molden, Wien-München-Zürich, 1969, translation copyright Allen Lane, 1973, reproduced by permission of Penguin Books Ltd.

Bach's *Chorale Prelude, Jesu, Joy of Man's Desiring*, arr. by Myra Hess, new and revised edition, 1931, Copyright and reproduced by permission of Oxford University Press.

Robert Donington's *The Interpretation of Early Music*, published 1963, reproduced by permission of Faber and Faber.

Ostinato from Mikrokosmos, Vol. VI (Bela Bartók) © Copyright 1940 by Hawkes & Son (London) Ltd.; Copyright Renewed. Reprinted by permission of Boosey & Hawkes, Inc.

MUSICAL EXAMPLES

NOTE: There are numerous references to examples which concern variants on the audiotape, without separate illustrations in the text (e.g., Ex. 7a, 7b).

MUSICAL EXAMPLES

MUSICAL EXAMPLES

MUSICAL EXAMPLES

Schubert, *Piano Sonata in D Major, Op. 53,* 4th mvt., Ex. 129, p. 90

Schubert, *Piano Sonata in A Major, Op. 120,* Andante, Ex. 64a, p. 51

Schubert, *Piano Sonata in A Minor, Op. 143,* 1st mvt., Ex. 53, p. 46

Schubert, *Symphony No. 9 in C Major,* 2nd mvt., Ex. 46, p. 43

Schubert, *Symphony No. 9 in C Major,* Finale, Ex. 47, p. 43

Schumann, *Arabesque,* Ex. 71, p. 57

Schumann, Die beiden Grenadiere, Ex. 136, p. 93

Schumann, *Kreisleriana,* 1st mvt., Ex. 108, p. 79

Schumann, *Piano Quintet,* 2nd mvt., Ex. 169, p. 115

Tchaikovsky, *Symphony No. 6 in B Minor, Op. 74, Pathétique,* 1st mvt., Ex. 10-11, pp. 16-17

Telemann, *Trio Sonata in C Minor,* 3rd mvt., Ex. 6, p. 10

Türk, *Klavierschule,* 1789, Ex. 60, p. 50

Wagner, *Tristan und Isolde,* Prelude, Ex. 130, p. 91

Weber, *Der Freischütz,* Wie nahte mir der Schlummer, Ex. 16, p. 22

Chapter One

INTRODUCTION

I remember a friend of some years ago whom I saw at almost every concert. He obviously was an avid music lover. He also was a very busy doctor who never had had the time to study music himself. One day he took me aside and confessed that he had enrolled in a piano class a while before. I said, "Congratulations, that's wonderful!" "Congratulations, my eye!" he answered. "I can't stand listening to myself, I sound so unmusical!"

When he started playing, the reason for his frustration became obvious. Every note was hammered out indiscriminately and the effect was decidedly painful. The mere suggestion, however, to check the accentuation of the words that went with the music (he played a folk song arrangement) made an enormous difference. In no time at all he started smiling as he listened to himself play.

This little episode brings out a simple but important fact: before we can sound musical[1] we have to know what sounds we want to produce, what to listen for. It is not enough to "play the notes." **We must have a concept of the music, an aural blueprint, so to speak, to which to match our performance.**

INADEQUACIES OF NOTATION: "FIXED" ELEMENTS AND VARIABLES

A score at first glance looks explicit enough; but notation alone does not begin to determine the subtler details of a performance. Pitches and time values are the only elements which are "fixed" and not subject to manipulation in performance. By contrast, **indications of tempo, dynamics, and articulation are only approximate. They are among the variables of performance, their exact levels and nuances determined only by the performer.** How fast is *andante*, how loud *piano*, how short *staccato*? Should all notes be equally loud when there are no marks of expression?

Once the performer begins to ask such questions, he has taken the first and most important step toward achieving a "musical" performance. Indeed, the adage, often quoted by mathematicians, "if we know the questions, we can find the answers," applies to a remarkable degree to musical interpretation.

Does the performer simply follow his instinct in dealing with such questions, or are there other, more objective factors to guide him? As we shall see, interpretation does involve both objective and subjective elements.[2]

---

[1]The word "musical" (as in "playing musically") is used a great deal but is not easily defined. After giving a ravishing peformance an artist will hardly consider it a compliment to be told that he "sounded musical." One would, of course, expect the performance of someone who deserves to be called an artist to be musical. The term "musical," however, does not in itself imply a high degree of artistry. What it does suggest is a performance which is, on the whole, convincing and enjoyable.

[2]*Objective*, as applied to musical performance: contained or implied in the score; arising from the musical context; *subjective*: entirely a matter of individual choice.

SOME COMMON MISCONCEPTIONS: OBSTACLES TO THE EFFECTIVE STUDY OF INTERPRETATION

For many musicians and music lovers musical interpretation is a matter of intuition and taste alone. There is even a certain mystique attached to interpretation. When asked to explain the magic of a breathtaking performance, many an artist will say, "I really don't know why I play the way I do; I just feel it this way." Nevertheless, a listener will scarcely like a performance he did not enjoy any better for knowing that the performer "felt it that way." Nor will a caring teacher, as a rule, let a student get away with a poor performance just because he "felt it that way."

It can be confusing to a performer trying to make up his mind about the interpretation of a particular piece to hear different fine artists interpret it quite differently. They may sound equally convincing and find equally enthusiastic approval with their audiences (as was the case with the pianists Horowitz, Rubinstein, and Serkin). The individual liberties taken and the greatly varying nuances in their performances only seem to enhance the fascination and enjoyment of the listeners. By contrast, less accomplished performers often sound merely unconvincing and the liberties they take, awkward and out of place.

There is no denying that these differences have a great deal to do with different levels of talent, temperament, and individual taste; but there is a danger in putting too much emphasis on talent and taste, both in the study and teaching of interpretation. A teacher may find it futile to try and teach a student he considers lacking in talent, and a student may only want to do "his own thing" rather than look for clues to musical interpretation beyond his personal taste and inclination.

The aims of teaching and study, however, must be to impart and acquire knowledge and skills irrespective of talent (which can neither be taught nor learned).[3] About taste one can not argue, as a familiar Roman proverb tells us (*De gustibus non est disputandum*). Performing "in good taste," however, generally has more to do with a knowledge of style than individual preferences.

Differences in the level and musicality of performances lie largely in the performers' grasp of the music and its interpretive requirements and implications. Performers who have gained the necessary insights in studying a score, and recognize and respect these requirements and implications, will not only be able to deal with the many variables successfully, but in their own individual fashion. Their interpretations may vary enormously; but they will neither sound unmusical nor run the risk of distorting the music.

---

[3]Dictionaries define "talent" as "mental endowment" and "natural ability." Accordingly, talent is a factor which is constant and cannot be "developed;" but it does play a significant role in the development of skills, both in the rate of progress and in the level of accomplishments attainable. It is up to the teacher to create the conditions in which talent can freely assert itself by offering the student the tools to develop a secure technique, a thorough understanding of the music, and helping to remove debilitating tensions.

INTRODUCTION

THE INTERPRETIVE PROCESS: THE "AREA OF APPROPRIATENESS" AND "INDIVIDUAL CHOICE"

To what extent is it possible to pinpoint what makes a passage sound "right" or "wrong," "musical" or "unmusical?" To be sure, the notions "right" and "wrong" apply only to the fixed elements: pitches are either right or wrong, and basic time values are rendered either correctly or incorrectly. Criteria for the variables are not nearly as clear-cut; but every score is full of clues which, properly observed, lead to convincing and "musical" performances. The following examples identify some of these clues.

The *sf* note in Example 1 must by definition stand out. It is obviously wrong not to make it louder than the surrounding notes; but to turn the simple *sf* into a *sfff* in the *piano* context of the example is also wrong. So somewhere between a gentle accent—its threshold above the level of the surrounding notes—and a vigorous but acceptable *sf* there is what we shall call an "area of appropriateness." This is illustrated in the following graph:

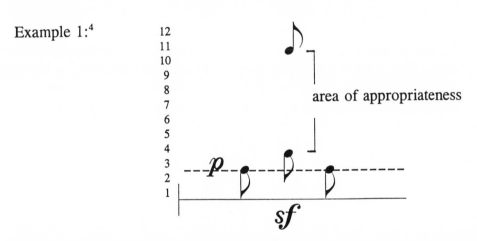

Below the lower limit of the area of appropriateness the *sf* does not fulfill its function; above the upper limit it sounds grossly exaggerated. Within its boundaries the performer chooses the level he likes best. And that is where individual preference enters the picture: a performer of gentle disposition will prefer Example 2a on the tape, one with a fiery temperament Example 2b.

---

[4]In the graph, the degrees of volume have been marked with numbers to make the differences more obvious.

Example 2: Beethoven, *Piano Sonata in G Major, Op. 14, No. 2*, 2nd Movement

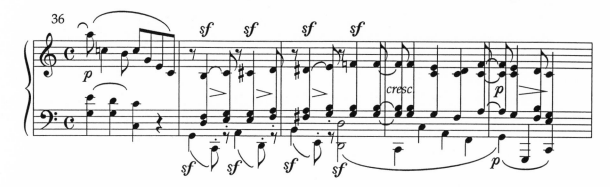

These examples serve as illustrations of the interpretive process applied to one element only, to dynamics. The following excerpts will do the same with regard to tempo and articulation. In each case the process is reduced to its bare essence: (1) the demarcation of **an area of appropriateness, which is determined by the musical context and therefore represents an objective element** (although its boundaries may vary slightly with different individuals); (2) **within that area of appropriateness the performer makes his own specific interpretive choice—subjectively, i.e., according to his taste and temperament.**

Example 3: Ravel, *Sonatine*, 3rd Movement

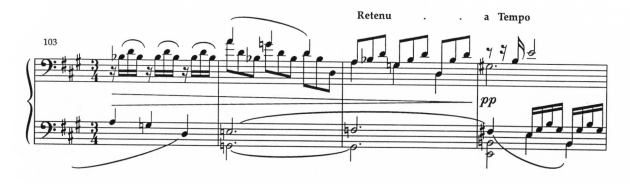

In the first taped version of Example 3 the *ritenuto (retenu)* has been suppressed (3a), in the second it leads to a virtual stop (3b). Both versions fall beyond the range of acceptable choices, and the area of appropriateness is again found within these extremes.

Example 4: Mozart, *Symphony No. 40 in G Minor*, K. 550, 2nd Movement

The flute has several notes of the same pitch in succession. As above, using extremes helps determine appropriate levels—in this case, degrees of articulation. In the first version on the tape each note is sustained to the point the separation can no longer be heard (Ex. 4a); in the second the notes are excessively short (4b).

DEALING WITH THE COMPLEXITIES OF INTERPRETATION

In addition to pinpointing the key elements of the interpretive process, the preceding examples also illustrate the most effective method of dealing with the complexities of interpretation, which is to address each element separately. In actual performance, of course, the various elements of music always appear in combination, even in a single melodic line: pitches and time values, volume and timbre, tempo and articulation, etc. A student may easily feel overwhelmed as he becomes aware of the complexities of musical interpretation. But if he ever went out for sports of any sort, he will have learned that methodical training invariably meant taking apart complex actions, and dealing at first with each component separately. Before a tennis player, e.g., can be sure to direct the ball to any intended spot, he has to understand —and practice separately—serving, forehand, backhand, racket angles for different trajectories, and patterns of steps to get into desired positions.

In elementary performance study the emphasis will generally be on the development of technical skills. But some elements of interpretation can and should be introduced in the earliest stages. To use another analogy: in learning how to read children are not expected to wait until they achieve the fluency of seasoned actors before putting accents on the proper syllables and observing punctuation. Similarly, **the music student should from the beginning be made aware of the fundamentals of accentuation and phraseology.**

There are many other analogies between speech and music. Indeed, **many phenomena of musical interpretation are more readily understood when compared to corresponding aspects of speech.** Since there are also numerous similarities in the training and performance of actors and musicians, analogies between speech and musical performance provide a valuable tool in the study of musical interpretation.

TEACHING MUSICAL INTERPRETATION

What does the teaching of musical interpretation entail? To begin with, **one might compare any teacher's basic function to that of a guide on a journey of discovery who points out what to look for and where to look.** Once the student has become aware of a phenomenon previously unknown or unnoticed, the teacher can further guide him in its examination and study until he thoroughly understands its nature and place in the scheme of things. Accordingly, the teaching of musical interpretation involves:

1. Helping the student discover and understand those elements which are subject to interpretation. These are essentially the "variables" described above, some of them spelled out with symbols and verbal indications such as *andante*, *p*, $>$, etc., others only implied in the musical context;[5]

2. Helping him define the kinds of adjustments the music calls for and the range of nuances appropriate in each case (within the "area of appropriateness"); and

3. Guiding him toward making the specific choices within that range of nuances which assure "musical" performances that bring out the essential character of the music and satisfy the listener while allowing him to follow his artistic impulse.

ACCURACY AND "MUSICAL" PERFORMANCE

The first and most obvious aim in the preparation of any piece for performance is accuracy: "learning the notes" and achieving a fundamental technical control. Merely rendering pitches and basic time values correctly, however, does not involve interpretation at all. We sometimes talk of "perfection" in a performance when all the notes are there, when there are no glaring rhythmic inconsistencies and a few of the most obvious requirements of expression and articulation have been met. At the same time we may feel let down, being vaguely aware that some vital ingredient is missing: **the mere absence of mishaps and a superficial perfection do not make for a truly musical performance**, let alone one that is arresting and evocative.

A conscientious performer will not be satisfied with mere mechanical responses to the notes and the markings in the score. He only becomes an "interpreter" as he deals with the variables knowingly and sensitively: tempo and tempo fluctuations, dynamics—i.e., the gradations and fluctuations of volume; articulation—the connection and separation of notes and their attack, shape and release, even varying the color of sounds produced.

A BOOK ON MUSICAL INTERPRETATION: BENEFITS AND LIMITATIONS

A book such as this is not intended to detract from the importance of the teacher. It cannot interact with the student. It can not react to the student's performance and come up with the suggestions appropriate at any moment. Neither can it spontaneously supply a model performance of any given passage as can the teacher.

---

[5]Especially the elements discussed in the chapters on Basic Musical Rhetoric and Musical Punctuation.

But it can—through explicit verbalization—identify and define the various elements of interpretation and help the student understand their nature and function. This does not necessarily occur in the traditional demonstration-imitation approach to teaching interpretation. **The intuitive processes involved in imitation do not in themselves assure learning;** for that to happen the mind of the student has to be actively engaged. Frequently, however, a student manages to imitate the teacher's demonstration quite satisfactorily, without knowing what made his performance successful. **Only if he has a solid grasp of the problems as well as the solutions involved can he apply what he has learned in mastering one piece to the performance of another.** In simple terms, **he must know *what* he did, *how* he did it, and *why!***

What has been said here is not meant to question the validity and importance of demonstration in the teaching of interpretation. In fact, the taped examples accompanying this book are an essential part of its pedagogy. The emphasis, however, must be on the kind of analytical approach which leads to a thorough understanding of the score itself and all that it implies.

The score represents the sum total of the composer's creation. It is the only embodiment of his intentions concerning the performance—explicit in his markings and implicit in his notation of the composition.[6]

BENEFITS OF THE SOCRATIC METHOD: ENGAGING THE STUDENT'S MIND

Only when a teacher asks questions can he be sure of the student's attention. Verbal instructions alone are not always fully understood and the student may obey the teacher and imitate his demonstration without really grasping what was being accomplished. But **in looking for appropriate answers to the teacher's questions the student has to think, his mind has to be engaged.** With the teacher's guidance he will also recognize the logic underlying the interpretation of a passage. At the same time he is bound to find it exhilarating to make these discoveries himself and infinitely more satisfying than blindly submitting to the teacher's authority or merely imitating what he has heard. In the process he will gain confidence; for there can be no greater assurance than that based on knowledge acquired through one's own probing and exploration.

Systematically put, the teacher's questions will cover all interpretive facets of a piece. Once the student has answered all of them, he will have created for himself the interpretive blueprint contained in the score and in effect have retraced the composer's intentions.

---

[6]Only rarely have composers written about the performance of their own works. The comments of their contemporaries concerning their performances and the annotations of editors represent observations and opinions colored by their own individual perceptions. While such "secondary" sources may be helpful to a degree, only a careful examination of the score—the "primary" source—will allow the performer to come face-to-face with the composer, so to speak, and grasp his intentions by retracing his steps in creating the work.

Consistently applied over a longer period, the teacher's Socratic approach sets a pattern the student is likely to follow. As a result he will, almost from force of habit, use the teacher's catalog of questions when facing a new score. In the process he will on his own arrive at a thorough grasp of the interpretive requirements.

INDIVIDUAL CHAPTERS' INVENTORIES OF COMMON INTERPRETIVE PROBLEMS

The various areas of interpretation are discussed in separate chapters. Each element within a particular area is in turn examined individually, separated from all others. The result is that each element can be clearly identified and dealt with confidently and conclusively.

Each chapter serves as an inventory of representative problems of interpretation. From that inventory the student can make up the list of questions which are pertinent to the piece under consideration, and the answers to the questions together will provide a satisfactory interpretive scheme. The use of such a checklist can be compared to a pilot's map and instrument checkoff before take-off. After every item has been checked, the flight has been fully plotted, with efficiency and safety assured.

Applied to musical performance such an approach prevents haphazard and inappropriate patterns which are difficult to correct once they are established. Therefore the process described above should be initiated in the earliest stages of preparation for performance. Unfortunately many students are in the habit of learning their music by playing a piece over and over, without analysis or planning. While the notes may ultimately be rendered accurately and the performance become reasonably polished, much time and effort can be saved if the piece is from the start systematically examined with respect to the various elements of interpretation—tempo, dynamics, articulation, etc. The arrangement of the material in the various chapters of the book provides a ready framework for such systematic examination.

ACTIVE LISTENING CRUCIAL TO EFFECTIVE PERFORMANCE

It should be taken for granted that a performer hears the sounds he produces. But just as on occasion we find ourselves *looking* without really *seeing*, so we may *listen* without *hearing*. Merely directing our eyes toward an object does not mean that we perceive it in all its detail, let alone its character and significance. Only an active, analytical, and penetrating kind of looking will assure that. As for listening, there are two points of the utmost importance of which a performer should be aware, once and for all:

1. The most artistic and musically impeccable concepts are of no use unless the performer is able to monitor the sounds he produces, assuring in the process that his concepts are translated into the corresponding sounds. In other words, he must hear his own performance as it progresses, constantly and automatically. (I still remember the shock, years ago, of realizing that the sounds which came

out of my piano did not at all match the exquisite tones I heard in my mind while playing.)

2.   For the listener each fragment of music only exists through the sounds which actually reach his ear. Only by monitoring his performance throughout can the performer assure that the sounds heard by the listener will match his musical and artistic intent.

It is vital that a student learn to listen to himself—and in the case of the aspiring conductor, to his ensembles—from the earliest possible stage. Then the monitoring process becomes an automatic and well-integrated part of his performance.

EXAMPLES OF COMMON PITFALLS: PERFORMING WITHOUT AN ADEQUATE "BLUEPRINT"

Example 5 illustrates what happens when someone just plays the notes and gives little thought to the interpretive implications of notation, rhythmic organization, and accentuation. All the examples of faulty or questionable versions of the passages included here were at some time or another actually heard in rehearsal or performance.

In a rehearsal of *Excerpts from Brigadoon* the first violins played

Example 5: Loewe, *Brigadoon*, The Heather on the Hill

with heavy downbows (⊓) and short and light upbows (V). Only after the conductor drew attention to the underlying familiar words was the bowing adjusted, with immediate, positive results.

Example 5a:

9

But even without consideration of the words it should have been obvious that the barring of the passage called for a typical ⁴⁄ accent scheme (primary accent on "1," secondary accent on "3," with the other notes, especially the sixteenths, deemphasized).

This is also a persuasive illustration of the fact that the technical aspects of the execution, here the bowing, have to be adjusted to the musical concept. To look at the problem in another way, **the musical concept must always determine the mechanics of execution, not vice versa.**

"MISHEARING" BY THE LISTENER AND HOW TO AVOID IT

The examples below have been included in order to show how easily the listener may misconstrue the rhythmic organization of a musical idea unless the performer brings out the pattern of accents clearly and unequivocally.

Example 6: Telemann, *Trio Sonata in C Minor*, 3rd Movement

The first version of the initial motive (Example 6a) imitates a commercial recording released some time ago. The barlines in the score (Example 6), however, suggest the version shown in Example 6b. Putting words—with their built-in accents—with the notes points up the distinction:

Example 6a: Example 6b:

to be sure   penetrate

10

INTRODUCTION

"Penetrate" fits the pattern of the original, "to be sure" does not. Reading the words with their accents reversed (tó bĕ súre and pĕnétrăte)[7] is obviously incorrect. But so is Version 6a on the tape. This is not a matter of individual taste or interpretation; it is wrong in view of the placement of the bars, by the composer!

The next example on the tape (bars 1 and 2 of Example 6) upon casual listening seems quite acceptable. On playing the example over, however, the listener will notice that it can be construed in two contradictory ways:

Example 6c:

Example 6d:

Only a sufficiently pronounced accentuation will prevent "mishearing" and assure that the listener grasps the pattern set down by the composer.

Some adjustments in the articulation will further assure that the phrase will be heard correctly: the eighth notes should be shortened, thus: 𝄽 and the first eighth note of bar 2 should be accented and preferably slurred to the quarter (as *appoggiatura* and resolution). The last eighth note of bar 2 should then be unaccented and shortened, thus: to point up its separation from bar 3, where a repeat of the same figure begins.

Example 6e:

Almost any music lover can remember instances of enjoying a performance when suddenly he felt tripped up, so to speak. The examples discussed show how a listener may

---

[7]The symbols ／ and ⌣ will be used throughout to designate accented and unaccented notes and syllables.

11

easily misconstrue the patterns he hears, and how the performer can with relatively little effort avoid ambiguities and distortions.

Example 7 also illustrates the need for care in providing the proper rhythmic orientation for the listener. It can actually be construed in three different ways. (For the sake of our examination the barlines have been omitted.)

Example 7: Beethoven, *Piano Sonata in G Major, Op. 14, No. 2*, 1st Movement

In the first version heard on the tape (Example 7a) the upward octave skip, followed by the descending figure, produces an accent on the second 16th note, which sounds rather satisfactory. The second version (7b) seems even more convincing, because the figure of five sixteenth notes here is heard as a unit, leading to the longer and weightier dotted eighth, bolstered by the entrance of the bass. But it is the third version (Example 7c), which turns out to be the one the composer intended.

Example 7c:

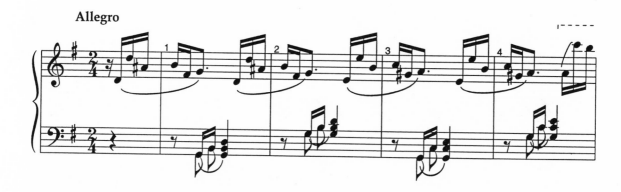

It sounds not only more graceful, but the bar lines allow no other interpretation, and the continuation of the initial passage, in bar 5, with its unmistakable, strong bar accent proves the point. A careless performer will inadvertently begin with versions 7a and 7b, only to have the listener jolted by the musical "hiccup" at bar 5, in which the continuation marked by the bracket ┌ ‑ ‑ ‑ ‑ ┐ seems to come at the wrong time.

Chapter Two

DYNAMICS

THE TERM "DYNAMICS"

According to the dictionary, "dynamics" refers to degrees of loudness and softness, as well as the "marks of expression," such as *p, f, dim.*, etc. There are, of course, other elements which contribute to making music "expressive;" but since there is no sound without volume, **dynamics are a constant factor in all musical performance.** Indeed, the degree of volume and the infinite range and variety of shading to which we apply the term "dynamics" greatly determine the quality of a performance.

It is interesting to discover upon examining dynamic markings that as a rule composers use them only to determine general levels of volume, the gradual changes between them, and special, characteristic accents. They almost never indicate the subtler dynamic inflections which are part of every motive and every phrase, inflections which are analogous to the syllabic and word accents of speech. The phenomena of this "basic musical rhetoric" are discussed in a separate chapter.[1]

The composers' dynamics are superimposed, so to speak, on the general musical context, much as a speaker dramatizes his delivery by raising his voice, thundering, whispering, or emphasizing key words in his message, all without changing the basic syllabic stresses.

The following well-known example is recorded in two versions in order to emphasize the powerful effect of these "superimposed" dynamics (Example 8a on the tape). The second version (8b), in which all printed dynamics are deliberately ignored, is dull and lifeless by comparison.

Example 8: Beethoven, *Piano Sonata in C Minor, Op. 13, Pathétique*, 1st Movement

---

[1]See Chapter Three.

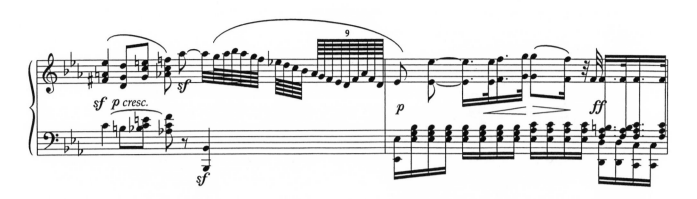

INTERPRETING DYNAMIC MARKS

Every musical idea has a character of its own, and the "marks of expression" supply the dynamic framework. The full spectrum of dynamics ranges from barely audible to deafening, and it is vitally important that the performer find the appropriate volume for each passage and, ultimately, each note.[2]

A few principles and ground rules will help in translating the printed markings into meaningful music-making faithful to the intentions of the composer.

Dynamic levels, from the softest *pp* to the loudest *ff* should be related to the general character of a work, as well as its style and period. A *ff* in Haydn or Mozart will be vastly different from a *ff* in Liszt, Strauss, or Mahler.

Special accents (*fp* , *sf* , $\wedge$, $>$, etc.) also must be adjusted to the surrounding context, in terms of both level and duration.[3] In addition, one should consider the dynamic range of the voice(s) and instrument(s) involved.[4] Even the acoustics of a hall and the circumstances under which a performance takes place must be taken into account.

It is most helpful to learn to think of dynamic levels in terms of a numerical scale.[5]

In Example 9 only one dynamic level is indicated, *pp* , apart from the signs $\longleftarrow$ and $\longrightarrow$. But as can be heard on the tape, an idiomatic and thoughtful interpretation will bring out a wealth of dynamic subtleties. The relative volume of notes is indicated here by means of a numbering system along a scale from 1 to 20.

---

[2]Occasionally, one finds episodes marked *senza espressione*, in which dynamic differentiation is avoided.

[3]See Chapter Six, p. 80.

[4]One must not only consider the relative power of instruments in an ensemble, e.g., trumpet and flute, but also the dynamic idiosyncrasies of individual instruments which may be powerful in a certain range of their compass, and weak in another.

[5]In trying to assign numerical values to dynamic levels along a sufficiently wide scale (1 to 20 or even 1 to 50) one becomes aware of nuances one would never think of when limiting oneself to the common marks of expression. See also Chapter Nine, p. 133.

Example 9: Debussy, *Reflets dans l'eau*

The common markings of *pp* , *p* , *mp* , *mf* , etc., are not really adequate when it comes to suggesting subtler gradations of volume. Even an occasional indication of *pppp* or *ffff* , probably meant by the composer to spur the performer's imagination rather than to be taken literally[6] can be more easily translated into practical dynamic values by means of a numerical system.

Example 10: Tchaikovsky, *Symphony No. 6 in B Minor, Op. 74, Pathétique,* 1st Movement

The indication *pppppp* can only be interpreted as an exhortation on the part of the composer to play as softly as humanly possible.

Many performers tend to play or sing *piano* as soon as they see the word *diminuendo* and, conversely, *forte* at the first glimpse of a *crescendo*. One must condition oneself to maintaining the prevailing dynamic level right up to the spot at which the *crescendo* or *diminuendo* is marked.[7] As the terms imply, *crescendo* and *diminuendo*—which are grammatically participles of the present tense—must always be gradual. This must be carefully   monitored, especially in extended passages marked *poco a poco crescendo* or

---

[6]In a rehearsal of *Otello* with the NBC Symphony Orchestra, Toscanini demanded a full-bodied *piano* from the strings in a passage marked *ppp* by Verdi . . . "He explained that the Italian orchestras for whom Verdi scored his works played everything in an unvarying *mezzoforte*, which forced the composer to write extremes for *forte* and *piano* in order to obtain nuances of any kind." (Quoted from *The Composer's Advocate*, by Erich Leinsdorf, p. 200.)

[7]Richard Lert, the noted teacher of orchestras and conductors, often scolded: "*Crescendo* means *piano* and *decrescendo* means *forte*!"

diminuendo. It is helpful to identify and mark intervening dynamic levels in order to avoid reaching a climax, or its opposite, too soon.

A *piano subito* should be treated as a dramatic event, not just as a change from one decibel level to another. Actually it usually occurs just when the unsuspecting listener would expect the climax of a *crescendo* passage. Its impact is the more powerful, the greater the element of surprise. Therefore the performer must guard against weakening its effect by an inadvertent *diminuendo*.

More often than not it is necessary after a *forte* climax to allow for a moment of silence before the sudden *piano* in order to let the reverberation dissipate. This can be done by shortening a note or, if that seems appropriate, by inserting a short rest, which would delay the beat ever so slightly, but usually without adverse effect.[8]

The words *crescendo*, *diminuendo*, etc., and the markings ⟍⟋ and ⟋⟍ are relatively crude and in exact when it comes to pinpointing the subtler dynamic nuances which are part of every fine performance. There are also instances in which, upon closer examination, one discovers that the composer or copyist may have been careless in the positioning of these markings. Therefore a *crescendo* mark sometimes does not jibe exactly with the group of notes or the part of a phrase for which it was intended. Upon closer examination and some experimentation the performer should be able to correct such discrepancies.

Example 11:   Tchaikovsky, *Symphony No. 6 in B Minor, Op. 74, Pathétique*, 1st Movement[9]

DYNAMICS IN CONTRAPUNTAL MUSIC

Composers of the Renaissance and Baroque periods used almost no dynamic markings. In dealing with fugues and other imitative counterpoint performers vary widely in their approach, from making every entrance of a subject very loud and leaving all the rest subdued, to making little or no dynamic differentiation. But the structure of the fugue itself and the traditional designation of its features furnish clues for a useful and convincing dynamic scheme. The main subject or principal motive dominates as the most conspicuous structural element, the countersubject or other material of secondary importance is made less prominent, and the rest of the texture, including episodic material, is further subordinated. If, in addition, the performer

---

[8]See the discussion of such pauses in Chapter Four.

[9]Example 11 is an exact copy of an edition which has had wide circulation.

remembers to keep all dynamic strands in balance, he will highlight the main features and achieve both clarity and contrast while avoiding exaggeration.

Example 12: J. S. Bach, *The Art of the Fugue,* Fuga VIII a 3 voci[10]

The terrace dynamics of the Baroque period are best understood in the light of the nature and limitations of the Baroque organ. Lacking the enclosed swell box and other devices of modern organs, it can not produce *crescendo* or *diminuendo*. Increases or decreases in volume are therefore brought about by adding or subtracting stops, resulting in an effect illustrated in the graph below:

Example 13:

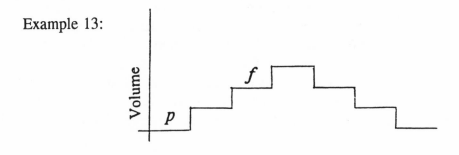

---

[10]The dynamics *f* , *mf* , and *mp* are added in keeping with the levels of prominence outlined above: fugue subject and answer, countersubject when it appears, and episodic material.

This scheme, also applied in ensemble music in general, manifests itself in the design of Baroque *concerti* in which solo instruments alone or combined in a *concertino* are opposed to the full orchestra, the *ripieno*. The effect is, to begin with, that of a deliberate juxtaposition of *piano* and *forte* and, when instruments are added in varying stages, that of the terrace dynamics described. In the juxtaposition of *forte* and *piano*, and especially the softer repetition of identical passages ("echo"), the temptation is great to exaggerate. As usual, some experimentation will help in determining the most satisfactory degree of contrast.

"NOT SEEING THE FOREST FOR THE TREES"

In order to allow a larger work to make its proper impact and to assure continuity and flow, the attention devoted to all smaller details must be balanced by a broader perspective. The old adage of the forest and the trees applies here, too. In practical terms this means looking for the focal points and dynamic climaxes of the various segments of the piece or movement in question.[11] The resulting perspective may be compared to a series of mountain ranges leading to and from a summit. Once the broader dynamic contour has been established, with all the various climaxes and adjustments between them clearly outlined, the haphazard, overly frequent and excessive dynamic swells ("overphrasing") can be avoided which sentimentalize and weaken the performance of even a powerful masterpiece.

VERTICAL BALANCES

Any time two or more tones are sounded simultaneously, questions of balance arise. Where two tones only are sounded together they tend to be equal in volume, unless one of them is clearly part of the melody or principal voice, in which case it should stand out. When there are three or more tones involved, the order of prominence normally will be (a) melody, (b) bass, (c) middle voice(s). If the melody note is in the middle or the bass, it should dominate, of course. The rest should then be adjusted so that the resultant sonority is satisfactory.

The following excerpt illustrates a common and satisfactory dynamic stratification: the top line dominates, the bass is slightly subordinated but clearly defined, and the triplets are kept very soft, merely supplying a kind of shimmering pulsation.

---

[11]See also Chapter Seven, p. 108.

Example 14: Schubert, *Impromptu in G Major, Op. 90, No. 3*

When a melodic line is doubled at the interval of an octave, it generally sounds better if one of the voices is louder. This approach is virtually implied in orchestral scoring where the bass routinely doubles the cello, subtly enhancing its sonority. Similarly, oboe and flute often move in octaves, with the flute providing a gentler overtone to the gutsier oboe. Having either the higher or the lower tone of an octave dominate, depending on the context and the judgment of the performers, invariably enhances the sonority. This is equally true in instrumental and vocal music and large and small ensembles as well. In piano music, too, the sound of octaves played in this fashion is preferable.

When there are several independent lines—in other words, in the case of contrapuntal treatment—each individual line has its own horizontal dynamic scheme which should be carefully observed while the parts are adjusted for vertical balance and transparency. The simplest method of ensuring that the theme or dominant line will stand out is to make all other lines softer. Sometimes it will be helpful to have the main line played or sung louder than indicated. Any problem can be almost eliminated through editing and marking of the adjusted levels in all parts concerned.

Even in the best-trained performing ensembles the uniform dynamic markings in the scores of composers of the classic and earlier periods will produce problems of balance.[12] A *forte* in the trumpet will simply obliterate the flute when both play in the same range. The only way to achieve balance and transparency is to adjust all markings and then fine-tune the ensemble in rehearsal, with the conductor's ear as the guide.

Pieces of homophonic music usually sound full and rich when each chord is properly balanced. The temptation is great to aim for the same kind of solid balance in polyphonic music, with less than happy results. In that case the music actually tends to sound muddy and ponderous, because the dynamic equalization impairs the delightful give and take of counterpoint. As suggested before, a thorough analysis of each line and a careful weighing of the relative importance of each contrapuntal strand will contribute immeasurably toward a transparent and stylish performance.

In certain passages—notably in music for large ensembles—one group of instruments or voices may have to hold a long note against moving parts. The result will often be that the long notes cover the more important melodic activity unless the singers and players concerned reduce the volume immediately after the initial attack.

---

[12]For an example of a score with uniform dynamic and accent markings, from top to bottom, and adjustments for better balance, see Chapter Six.

Example 15:   Beethoven, *Symphony No. 5 in C Minor, Op. 67*, 4th Movement[13]

---

[13]I have added the markings in parentheses to indicate the approximate adjustments the players of the parts concerned must make. Otherwise, cellos, basses, and contrabassoon from bar 86 on, and the second violins in bar 88, would barely be heard, if at all.

When a score is analyzed and treated in the manner outlined above, the performance will invariably be more transparent and altogether more satisfying. The process is slow and laborious but in itself rewarding in view of the insights and the more thorough understanding it affords. It is also the only means toward achieving a satisfactory performance reflecting as closely as possible the intentions of the composer.[14]

MELODIC DIRECTION AND DYNAMICS

There appears to be a "law of dynamics" which calls for *crescendo* when the pitchline rises and *decrescendo* when it falls. On the face of it this seems all wrong; but in many cases it is clearly borne out. A singer will almost automatically make a *crescendo* as he sings an ascending scale, and a *diminuendo* as he goes down.

Example 16: Weber, *Der Freischütz,* Wie nahte mir der Schlummer

This is a beautiful example of an undulating melody, with the inflections in volume corresponding to the melodic contour. On wind instruments the same phenomenon can be observed and even string players seem to do this quite naturally.

---

[14]The performer should take note of all signs or indications by the composer. It is then up to him to "interpret" them or, in the absence of markings, let the context determine the interpretive inflections.

In the absence of explicit instructions by the composer it is, of course, impossible to be certain of his intentions. The performer, however, may safely make the following assumptions:

1. Most composers, and certainly those of acknowledged genius and skill, are likely to have known precisely what they were about. It seems inconceivable that they would have condoned outright imbalance and muddiness, careless and illogical articulation, and exaggerations of all kinds.

2. If a passage appears incongruous or puzzling to the performer, the reason lies probably in some misunderstanding on his part rather than a lapse or lack of skill and discrimination of the composer.

3. If composers' markings are less than exact or "questionable," that is due (a) to the prevailing practices of earlier periods, (b) to their apparent assumption that the performer would be able to deal "musically" with the interpretive requirements of the score, and (c) to their unwillingness to limit a performer's artistic freedom.

Example 17: Mozart, *Sonata for Violin and Piano in B Flat Major, K. 378,* 1st Movement

In this version the editor has added markings which, however, only bear out the dynamic adjustments the melody seems to call for anyway.

A special effort is required—particularly in singing—to counteract this tendency and keep the dynamic level even. The effect, however, can be striking and usually serves a specific dramatic purpose.

Example 18: Bizet, *Carmen,* La fleur que tu m'avais jetée[15]

One important point should be included here even though it involves tone color as well as dynamics: many singers and instrumentalists tend to produce a rough or forced sound in *forte* and a lifeless or breathy one in *piano.* Variety of color is, of course, most desirable; but it should be achieved irrespective of dynamic levels. In other words, a gentle sound need not be lifeless or flabby. There can even be great intensity in *piano,* as in a fine actor's stage whisper, and beauty and a relaxed, noble kind of power in *forte.* As in all areas of interpretation, this is a matter of concepts: once the performer has established a mental image of the preferred tone colors, the means to obtain them can be found quite readily.

---

[15]The high range of this passage makes many tenors ignore the *pp* and turn it into a conventional *f* climax. As Martial Singher puts it in his perceptive comments, Don José "sings an aria of devotion, of torment, of remorse, of passionate love, ending with total capitulation, delivering himself into Carmen's hands: *'j'étais une chose a toi'* (*I was a thing belonging to you*)! . . . The dynamics *must* be *pianissimo* here. Don José has turned himself into the antihero, and a heroic B-flat is a bit of painful nonsense, even if the public demands it." (Quoted from *An Interpretive Guide to Operatic Arias.*)

Chapter Three

BASIC MUSICAL RHETORIC[1]

Anybody who has ever had music lessons or introductory music classes knows the meaning of "time signature," "measure," "meter," "barline," etc. As a rule, these fundamentals of music are clearly defined in music dictionaries and books dealing with musical basics. Any performance, however, involves a number of elements which are not included among those fundamentals and which usually are not even mentioned in music dictionaries or books on the fundamentals of music.

FUNDAMENTALS OF PERFORMANCE

This entire chapter is devoted to the purpose of identifying some of those "fundamentals of performance," which are implied but not specifically spelled out in musical notation, as well as some of the keys to interpretation contained in every score.

To begin with, let us draw attention to a significant phenomenon of musical performance which is best understood by way of its analogy to speech. One can distinguish two levels of speech: a basic one, with a normal tone of voice and a neutral kind of delivery which allows the general meaning of the words to come across, and a second one, which is superimposed on that basic level of delivery and carries the interpretation of the content, chiefly by means of raising and lowering the voice and varying pace and articulation.

Example 19: Hans Christian Andersen, *The Real Princess,* excerpt, recorded in two versions, "neutral" (19a on the tape) and "interpretive" (19b).

> The next morning she was asked how she had slept. "Oh, very badly indeed!" she replied. "I scarcely closed my eyes the whole night through. I do not know what was in my bed, but I had something hard under me, and am all over black and blue. It has hurt me so much!"

In the performance of music two such levels of delivery can also be distinguished: a basic level which allows the essential nature and organization of musical patterns to come across, and a second level, also superimposed on the first, which reflects the composer's marks of expression as well as the performer's interpretation.

---

[1]In the *Encyclopædia Britannica* (14th ed.), rhetoric is defined as "the art of using language in such a way as to produce a desired impression on the hearer . . ." Delivery is an essential part of rhetoric. In view of the far-reaching analogies between speech and musical performance, the notion of a "musical rhetoric" seems quite valid. The word "basic" has been added to denote the basic level of delivery addressed in this chapter.

Example 20: Beethoven, *Bagatelle, Op. 33, No. 1*

Example 20a on the tape represents the second, the interpretive level described above, which reflects Beethoven's marvelous capricious dynamics. Version 20b, in which all marks of expression are disregarded, sounds bland and uninteresting by comparison; but upon listening carefully one realizes that this "neutral" version is not entirely mechanical nor really unmusical. In fact, **it is the manner in which the performer deals with this basic level of delivery which largely determines the musicality of his performance.** The area of performance discussed here is generally given little attention, if any, and no separate term even exists to identify it. In using the designation "musical rhetoric" we follow a notable precedent.[2]

DYNAMIC INFLECTIONS WITHOUT DYNAMIC MARKINGS

The examples below contain no dynamic marks except for the *p* at the beginning which merely sets a general level of volume. Yet on the tape one hears dynamic inflections throughout each example, which not only do not disturb but are a vital and integral part of the performance.

Example 21: Haydn, *Piano Sonata in F Major (1773)*, 1st Movement

---

[2]In his book *Phrasing and Articulation*, Hermann Keller frequently draws attention to analogies between speech and music. Its subtitle reads: "A Contribution to the Rhetoric of Music."

Example 22: Chopin, *Prelude in A Major, Op. 28, No. 7*

One important aspect of this phenomenon can again be best explained by way of the analogy of musical performance to speech. A line of text may be read in many different ways, depending on the concepts of the actor or speaker. One element, however, will always remain constant: the pattern of syllabic accents. The word "father" for example—with the accent on the first syllable—will never become "fathér," or the word "grandfather," "grandfáther," or "grandfathér." When the difference between accented and unaccented syllables is not maintained, the delivery becomes monotonous. The words become almost unintelligible and for the listener the meaning of the text is all but lost.

MUSICAL IDEA DEFINED BY DISPOSITION OF ACCENTS

A musical idea, too, has its pattern of accents. Without them it tends to sound inane and mechanical. Unlike the fixed, built-in accents of polysyllabic words, however, their location in a group of notes varies, depending on a number of factors.

It should be noted that the actual difference in volume between accented and unaccented syllables is very slight. So is the difference between the accented and unaccented notes of a phrase not containing special accents (such as *sf*, *fp*, $>$, etc.). **In either speech or music, however, these accents and the corresponding subtle dynamic inflections are a crucial and essential part of every utterance.**[3] This is more obvious with speech, which has the purpose of communicating the meaning of words. A musical idea—a motive, a phrase, or any configuration of notes—may be assumed to have meaning, too. That "meaning," however, unlike that of words with their specific denotative capacity, has to do with the design and structure of the musical idea and its character and mood. **It is mainly the disposition of**

---

[3]Joseph Kerman writes in *Listen* (p. 5): "No single feature of music, not even the melody, determines the effect of music more crucially than the timing and weighting of notes: duration and accents."

accents which defines the musical idea, and any change in their quality and location affects its character. The factors on which their location depends will be discussed here in some detail, especially since none of these accents are normally marked with any of the common accent symbols (∧ , > , *sf* , *fp*, etc.).

To begin with, we must remember that our ear perceives the pulse or beat underlying all music in groups of twos or threes.[4] In a 2-beat group the accent may fall on the first or the second beat, in a 3-beat group on the first, second, or third, thus:

Example 23:

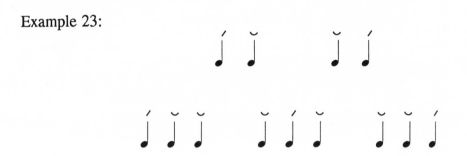

Putting words to these groups of notes helps to point up the difference:

Example 24:

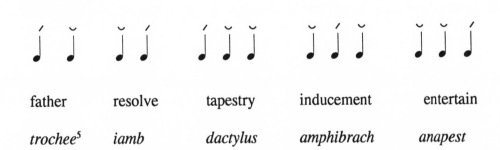

father	resolve	tapestry	inducement	entertain
trochee[5]	*iamb*	*dactylus*	*amphibrach*	*anapest*

In order to avoid confusion with the regular marks of expression, the signs / and ∪ are used here and elsewhere in this book to indicate accented and unaccented beats which are normally not marked at all.[6] The notes themselves look exactly alike, of course, and among

---

[4]Concerning groups of four or more beats, see p. 31.

[5]In these examples we have also introduced some of the elements of Greek prosody which are helpful in identifying the structure and accent patterns of musical motives. See Grosvenor Cooper and Leonard Meyer, *The Rhythmic Structure of Music*.

[6]In addition to the accent symbols / and ∪ the following signs are also used in the book: ▮ and ⊘ . Their order of prominence from loud to soft is ▮ ⊘ / ∪ .

many performers there is a decided tendency to make them sound alike, too. This may be due to a lack of knowledge and experience, as in the case of younger players, or a reluctance even among more mature performers to use dynamic nuances when the score does not specifically call for them.

It cannot, however, be emphasized enough that **two adjoining notes never are quite even. One is accented, the other not**, just as in normal speech no two adjoining syllables are ever truly even. To be sure, when several or many short notes follow one another at a fast pace, they may require a certain dynamic evenness. Upon closer examination, however, it becomes clear that they, too, are subject to dynamic adjustments which are determined by the underlying beat pattern, the rhythmic skeleton of the passage.

Example 25: Schubert, *Impromptu in E Flat Major, Op. 90, No. 2*

Due to the fast pace of this excerpt the dotted half (𝅘𝅥𝅭) is felt as the basic beat, with four ¾ measures grouped into one larger measure (12/4). The ¾ pattern then becomes a subdivision of the larger beat.

Example 26:

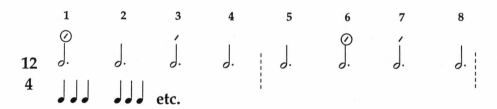

28

In the second "larger measure" the main accent seems to fall on bar 6, rather than on bar
5. This phenomenon is further discussed in Chapter Seven.

FUNCTION OF THE BARLINE IN FIXING BASIC ACCENTS

In musical notation it is generally the barline which indicates the accented beat of a group, the "downbeat" or "strong" beat of a measure.

Example 27:

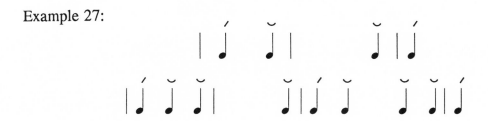

The following groups of five eighth notes and an eighth rest illustrate quite conclusively how the placement of the barline determines the accent of each group.

Example 28:

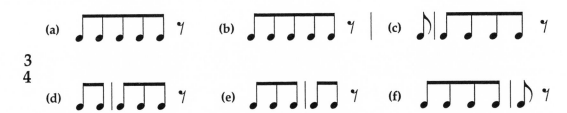

Example 28a, with the barline omitted, represents merely a group of undifferentiated equal eighth notes. Only the placement of the barline establishes an accent and with it the focal point of the group. In order to emphasize the considerable differences between these examples, due only to the shift of the barline, words have been put with the notes:

Example 29:

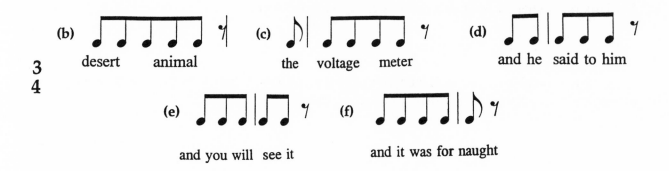

3
4

(b) desert   animal

(c) the   voltage   meter

(d) and he   said to him

(e) and you will   see it

(f) and it was for naught

As we play these notes or say the words, we sense a flow toward the accented note or syllable. In addition, we may observe that the notes group themselves around the accent in such a way that there is a hint of a *crescendo* toward the accent and a corresponding *decrescendo* away from it. These dynamic nuances are implicit in these groupings. In the absence of dynamics marked by the composer, however, they remain quite subtle. To add dynamic marks (⬍ and ⬍ or *crescendo* and *decrescendo*) would only lead to exaggerations.

The examples below illustrate again how significantly the placement of the barline, the assignment of different time signatures and the corresponding meter changes affect the accent scheme. While the series of time values remains entirely unchanged, the character of each rhythmic configuration resulting from the shift in barlines substantially differs from the next.

Example 30:

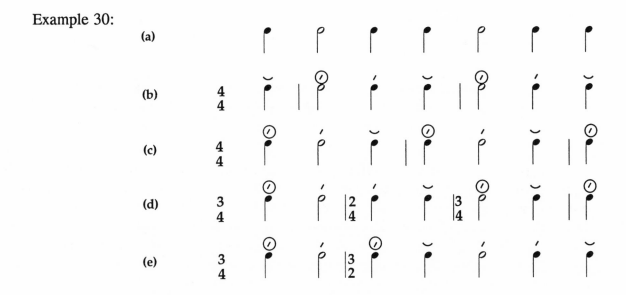

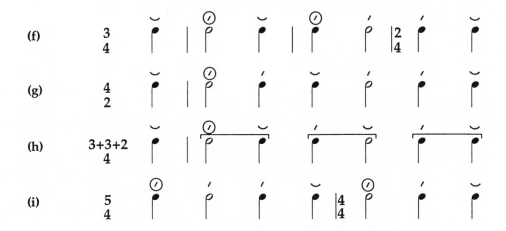

In many simple tunes or pieces of music the meter will be constant in a succession of repeated 2-beat or 3-beat groups. One will notice, however, that **any two or more successive measures will group together in such a way that the accented beat of some measures will be more prominent than those of others.** This phenomenon is, to begin with, familiar from the combination of primary groups of two and three beats into larger ones, of four, five, six, etc.

In Example 31 the accents are differentiated and again marked with the symbols ⊘ for the heavier primary accent and / for the lighter secondary accent.

Example 31:

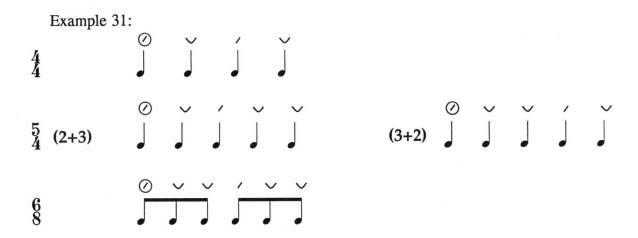

The following example serves as a reminder of **the basic "hierarchy of accents," which underlies any metric pattern** (primary and secondary accents on "1" and "3," "2" and "4" being unaccented, and still less emphasis on the intervening eighth notes).

31

Example 32:

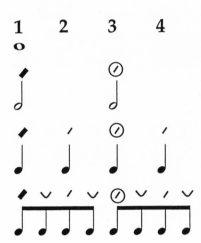

The "hierarchy" extends, of course, to smaller subdivisions (♫♫♫ and ♫♫♫ , etc.) and applies also, in similar fashion, to triple time.[7] It must be emphasized that **a repeated literal application of such a scheme—measure after measure—is deadly**, just like the kind of poetry reading mentioned above. But the scheme itself must never be ignored. When it is judiciously applied, it is most helpful in determining the relative weight of each note and, beyond that, in assuring an appropriate and convincing dynamic contour for each motive and each phrase.

SOME GROUP ACCENTS MORE PROMINENT THAN OTHERS: THE *GROSSTAKT*

The following examples further illustrate the tendency to perceive some groups of several measures as *Grosstakte* (*Grosstakt* being a term coined by the German musicologist Hugo Riemann which means "large measure").

---

[7]Triple-time "hierarchy":

Example 32b:

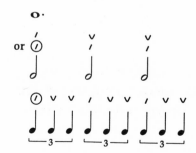

Example 33: Beethoven, *String Quartet in F Flat Major, Op. 74,* 3rd Movement

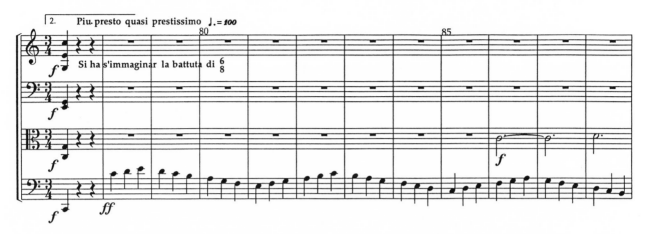

Beethoven's direction, in Italian, means: "here one must imagine a beat of $\frac{6}{8}$." Thus two measures of $\frac{3}{4}$ form a larger measure, actually in $\frac{6}{4}$, not $\frac{6}{8}$, with the stronger accent on the first of each two $\downarrow$ beats.

Example 34: Dukas, *The Sorcerer's Apprentice*

The second taped version of this theme in which the *Grosstakt* principle is applied (34b) is quite obviously preferable to the first (34a). In effect three measures of $\frac{3}{8}$ form one of $\frac{9}{8}$, according to the following accent scheme.

Example 34c:

While the normal accentual pattern in $\frac{4}{4}$ **is** **, there is a similar differentiation of weight in a *Grosstakt*. The order of emphasis, however, is most often reversed, the typical, most frequently encountered pattern being light-heavy-light-heavy (abbreviated l-h-l-h).**

Example 35:   Mozart, *The Marriage of Figaro*, La vendetta

Allegro con spirito

Bartolo

La   ven - det - ta,   oh,   la   ven   det - ta

l   h   l   h

Sometimes the order is h-l-l-h or even l-h-h-l, depending on the context. Various factors such as melodic contour, rhythmic patterns, and harmonic tension will determine which measure of the group receives the main emphasis. It should be added that as in the basic ¼ meter with its primary and secondary accents the "heavy" measures in the *Grosstakt* are usually not equal in weight.

FOCAL POINTS[8]

In examining this principle further, the analogy with language will again be helpful, as can be gathered from the sample of poetry below.

O, how much more doth beauty beauteous seem

By that sweet ornament which truth doth give!

The rose looks fair, but fairer we it deem

For that sweet odour which doth in it live.

(Shakespeare, *Sonnet LIV*)

The lines of Shakespeare's sonnet, composed in iambic pentameter, have each iamb marked (ᴗ∣). Giving each accent the same emphasis, as children usually do when reading poetry, sounds rather painful. If, however, one delivers the lines with their normal inflections, the accents marked ⊘ stand out, providing focal points for each line and allowing the meaning to come across more clearly. The other syllabic and word accents still remain, but fitted into the context in such a way that neither flow nor meaning are impaired.

---

[8]Focal points are more extensively discussed in Chapter Seven.

DYNAMIC IMPLICATIONS OF DURATIONAL VALUES

In addition to the phenomena described so far there is another element which has significant implications in terms of "basic rhetoric," that of durational values. The example below contains notes of different time values, from whole notes to sixteenths:

Example 36:

There are no barlines and no rhythmic organization beyond the durations of the notes themselves; but even if the notes are played without dynamic differentiation, the longer notes seem to stand out. Most performers will indeed tend to make the longer notes louder. The shorter, faster notes by comparison sound fussy unless played more softly.

The dynamic scheme indicated below will sound quite satisfactory. Numbers have been assigned to indicate different levels of volume.

Example 37:[9]

On the tape the first version (37a) is played on a sustaining instrument, the second (37b) on a kettle drum.

Applied with a grain of salt **the principle that long means heavy and short means light can be very useful in making a passage flow** and giving it a convincing dynamic contour.

METER NOT ALWAYS IN AGREEMENT WITH BARRING SCHEME

Barlines mark off measures, and time signatures indicate the prevailing meter. Frequently, however, the meter underlying the actual rhythmic organization of a passage does not agree with the measures or the barring scheme. It is essential that the performer recognize these deviations. The examples below illustrate the notation of such passages in which composers retain one time signature and barring scheme, usually in order

---

[9]Composers usually write notes of different time values for timpani and other percussion instruments even though the tone cannot be sustained and their volume diminishes at a rate beyond the performer's control. If the time values are to have any meaning, however, longer notes must be louder than shorter ones. In other words, the volume becomes a function of the duration.

to avoid frequent and often confusing changes in time signatures—while assuming the performer will recognize this and let the true rhythmic organization of a passage emerge in his performance.[10]

In the following example horns and basses continue in ⁶⁄₈ patterns, in accordance with the time signature; but the others have the sixteenth notes arranged in patterns of four and the 8ths in groups of two, thus in ²⁄₄. While the notes are beamed in groups of six, respectively, three, the melody clearly suggests groups of four and two. Thus each quarter receives an accent, and the secondary accent on the fourth eighth note, typical in ⁶⁄₈, is eliminated.

Example 38: J. S. Bach, *Brandenburg Concerto No. 1 in F Major*, 3rd Movement

Example 39: Monteverdi, *Canzonetta* Chiome d'oro

The meter of the violin parts can be construed in two ways: (1) in $\frac{3}{8}$ (marked by the broken vertical lines) or (2) in $\frac{3}{4}$ (marked with brackets).

The following example is particularly interesting, since the music at first sight suggests rhythmic schemes quite different from the sounds heard in performance.

Example 40: Copland, *El Salón México,* piano reduction

In Line 1 below the score is reduced to its rhythmic outline, with all accents included as marked by the composer. In Line 2 the notation is changed to represent the time values and groupings actually heard, i.e., the time signatures and groupings we would very likely write down if we heard the music without seeing the score.

Example 41:

Chapter Four

TEMPO

FINDING AND MAINTAINING THE "RIGHT" TEMPO

Hearing a passage played at different speeds makes one realize how much the tempo affects the character of the music. A difference of a few points on the metronomic scale will not matter greatly; but without some care a lively performance becomes frantic and a leisurely one tedious. Every performer, however, can quite easily find a suitable tempo by playing the passage in question at different speeds—from too fast to too slow. Invariably one tempo, or a relatively narrow range of tempos, will appear preferable to all others.

USING THE METRONOME

The metronome is, of course, very useful in the case of works furnished with the appropriate numbers.[1] When, however, there are no metronomic indications, either at the beginning of a work or for the various tempo changes occurring within it, the kind of experimentation described above can always be applied. Needless to say, the performer should mark down the appropriate metronome numbers once the respective tempos have been determined.[2]

TEMPO MARKINGS

The tempo markings found at the beginning of a piece—mostly in Italian, but frequently in the language of the composer—generally refer to the mood of the music rather than its speed (e.g., lively, *allegretto, heiter, animé*, etc.). The actual pace, and the corresponding metronome number, should therefore be carefully measured against the mood or character such an indication suggests.

Composers differ considerably in the use of terminology. It is helpful to familiarize oneself with any known comments concerning their own performance of their music and to study their use of tempo markings.[3] Some knowledge of the performance practices of the various historical periods is also desirable, particularly in the case of pre-classic music.[4]

Even composers and performers who were contemporaries did not always agree in

---

[1]The metronome, named after Johannes N. Maelzel, was actually invented in 1812 by the Dutchman Dietrich Nikolaus Winkel. When Winkel refused to sell the rights to his invention, Maelzel had the metronome patented in his own name. Beethoven was the first major composer to publish metronome indications for his works. The validity of such indications has often been questioned because of the inconsistencies in some composers' metronome numbers, as well as the known inaccuracies of metronomes owned and used by certain composers.

[2]One of the composers who was both meticulous and generous in this respect was Bartók, who usually indicated also the time elapsed in minutes and seconds.

[3]See Sachs, Curt, *Rhythm and Tempo.*

[4]See Donington, Robert, *The Interpretation of Early Music.*

matters of interpretation; but rather than ignoring composers' markings or rejecting historical information which may not appear unequivocal or completely reliable, one should use them for guidance and as points of departure. One might also keep in mind that in the matter of tempo, as in other areas of performance, there is a common-sense middle ground between fussy pedantry, on one hand, and carelessness and self-indulgence, on the other.

CLUES IN THE SCORE

What does the score itself reveal which can assist in determining an appropriate tempo?

A.   Limitations to speed implicit in the music:

1.   Technically demanding passages become virtually unplayable at excessive speeds, and configurations of fast notes tend to become blurred.[5]

2.   Certain figures, such as dotted groupings, require restraint, otherwise the rhythm is obscured.

Example 42: J. S. Bach, *French Suite No. 1 in D Minor,* Gigue

In keeping with accepted practice, the pick-up notes () are shortened on the tape (Ex. 42a).[6]
At excessive speeds the dotted figures may inadvertently be turned into triplets (Ex. 42b on tape):

---

[5]Mahler once said: "A tempo is right if everything comes across. If a figure can no longer be grasped by the ear because the sounds merge into one another, then the tempo is too fast. In the case of a *presto* the upper limit of distinction is the right tempo—beyond this it loses effectiveness." (Quoted in Kurt Blaukopf, *Gustav Mahler,* p. 189.) One might add that performers of extraordinary facility sometimes manage seemingly impossible speeds; but cramming the largest number of notes into the space of a second rarely makes for the most eloquent and meaningful music-making.
[6]See Donington, Robert, *op. cit.*

3. In pieces with one prevailing tempo the fastest passage will determine the top speed. Conversely, maintaining a minimal flow will help in avoiding an excessively slow pace. It must be stressed that slowing down in fast passages and speeding up in slow ones must be avoided, for this negates the very purpose of changes in figuration.

Example 43: J. S. Bach, *Brandenburg Concerto No. 4 in G Major*, 3rd Movement

At the proper tempo the fast notes of the solo violin add a touch of joyful exuberance. At the faster tempo they sound frantic (43a).

B. Indications by the composer:

At times one hears performances in which a composer's markings are ignored. Debussy's "Fêtes," the second of his orchestral *Nocturnes*, provides an interesting case in point. The opening, in C , is marked *Animé* (animated), the passage beginning in ⁶⁄₈ , *Plus animé* (more animated). The indications *très rhythmé* and *très marqué* also imply a slower tempo: the faster the triplets, the less "marked" they can be. Yet one almost always hears the opening, marked C , played very fast, *alla breve* (Ex. 44a), and the second passage slower or at best at the same tempo.

Example 44: Debussy, *Nocturnes*, Fêtes

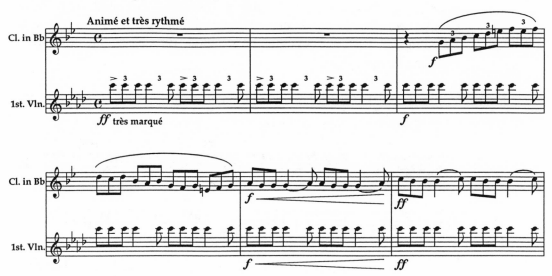

Example 45: Debussy, *Nocturnes*, Fêtes

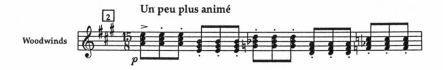

This has almost become a tradition, though obviously contrary to the composer's explicit instructions. Moreover, the musical results are questionable. In a moderately fast $\frac{4}{4}$ each triplet and each individual note can be heard clearly. The overall effect is one of vigor and excitement (Ex. 44b). When, however, the opening is played *alla breve*, the repeated notes seem to run together, almost creating a glib *tremolo*. Similarly, the woodwind passages are more interesting at a slower pace. Each note makes its point and the resulting figures have more substance and drive.

To mention one other well-known example: the tempo markings in Schubert's Ninth, the "Great" C-Major Symphony, are frequently ignored. The first movement is marked *Allegro ma non troppo*; yet one usually hears it played *Allegro molto*. One might add that most conductors make a pronounced *accelerando* in the Introduction which is in no way marked in the score and actually counteracts the build-up in texture and rhythmic intensity.[7] The wonderful effect of a release—both in tension and flow—at the start of the *Allegro ma non troppo* is thereby lost. The second movement often is played more slowly than its heading, *Andante con moto*, suggests, and the *Finale*, marked merely *Allegro vivace*, is generally played *presto* or *vivacissimo*.

---

[7]Of eight recorded versions examined only one avoids this *accelerando*.

Example 46:   Schubert, *Symphony No. 9 in C Major*, 2nd Movement

The *Andante con moto* on the tape is taken at the speed of MM ♪ = 116. Occasionally one hears the movement played at MM ♪ = 100, which makes it sound interminable.

Example 47:   Schubert, *Symphony No. 9 in C Major,* Finale, violins only

The tempo on the tape is MM ♩ = 96. Many conductors take speeds up to MM ♩ = 110.

C.   Apart from technical limitations, certain figures and passages allow for a faster pace, others require restraint:

   1.   Broken chords, or simple elaborations along the tones of a chord, as well as scale figures (Ex. 48) still sound satisfactory at speeds which seem too fast for "substantive" figures of non-chordal or non-scalar groupings (Ex. 49).

Example 48:   J. S. Bach, *The Well-Tempered Clavier,* Volume I, Prelude in C Sharp Major

Example 49: J. S. Bach, *French Suite No. 4 in E Flat Major,* Prelude

2.   A fast harmonic rhythm, too, has a restraining effect.

Example 50a: Beethoven, *Bagatelle, Op. 126, No. 5*

In this example the changes of harmony occur for the most part on each beat (♩.). However, the measures before the double bar have, respectively, two and three changes per ♩. beat, making the repeat without a relaxation of the tempo sound almost ludicrous (50b).

Example 51: Chopin, *Nocturne in E Flat Major, Op. 9, No. 2*

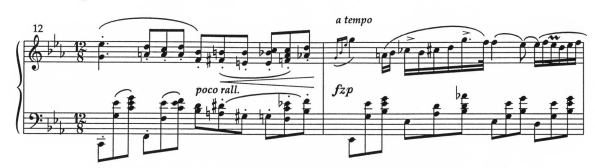

In this case the composer himself indicated the *rallentando* made necessary by the fast changes of harmony.

3. Passages in which chord progressions are broken up into contrapuntal figurations also seem to require a slower tempo.

Example 52: J. S. Bach, *English Suite No. 2 in A Minor,* Allemande

FACTORS AFFECTING TEMPO PERCEPTION

A listener's tempo perception depends not only on the actual metronomic speed, but also on other elements. In the following example the listener will have the impression of a tempo change. Actually the tempo and the beat remain constant; only the figuration changes as beats are subdivided or combined into larger durational values.

Example 53: Schubert, *Piano Sonata in A Minor, Op. 143*, 1st Movement

The greater the discrepancy in time values, the more the performer will be tempted to compensate for it and vary the basic beat. This tendency is one of the most common problems in all ensemble playing, only too familiar to conductors and chamber music and orchestra players.

The crisper the articulation, the greater the apparent speed. Even though the eighth notes in the following examples are equal in duration, the effect is still startlingly different. This is due in part to differences in the melodic design (disjunct motion in one, conjunct motion in the other), but primarily to differences in articulation; the *marcato* eighths are heard as separate beats, while the *legato* notes are heard in groups of three (as triplets), with one beat for each group.

Example 54: J. S. Bach, *St. Matthew Passion,* Sind Blitze, sind Donner

Example 55: J. S. Bach, *Chorale Prelude, Jesu, Joy of Man's Desiring,* arr. by Myra Hess

In vocal music, too, the degree of crispness affects tempo perception. The crisper the enunciation, the faster the pace will seem.

Even range and color will have some influence on the choice of tempos. A *Lied* can be sung faster by a light soprano than a contralto or bass. Similarly a lively tune played on the piccolo will sound grotesque if taken at the same speed on the tuba.

So far we have addressed the problem of finding the appropriate tempo for a given passage and of keeping a tempo constant in spite of changing figuration and articulation. Abrupt changes of tempo, which are usually marked by the composer (from *adagio* to *allegro*, e.g.), prove no more problematic than establishing any tempo. Of course, performers, and conductors especially, must condition themselves through practice to shifting from one tempo to another securely and without hesitation.

ACCELERATION AND RETARDATION

Apart from simple folk songs or dances there are few pieces of music which do not call for some deviations from a steady beat. Such deviations include, to begin with, increasing and decreasing the tempo, usually marked by the composer (*accelerando, stringendo, ritardando, allargando*, etc.). Most of these have a function and character which the composer Paul Hindemith tellingly defined by using the term *einleiten* (to introduce) for such transitional tempo adjustments. Generally such tempo changes are meant to be gradual[8], though by varying degrees of rapidity.

Some caution is in order here. Anyone remembers being thrown forward or pinned against the back of the seat while riding in a car, or even being jerked back and forth through careless braking and accelerating on the part of the driver. Uneven acceleration or deceleration in a performance has a comparably unpleasant effect on the listener. The performer must calculate the rate of acceleration or deceleration so that once a *ritardando* has begun, the process is not reversed until the new tempo has been reached or the piece is concluded. This is particularly important in long passages marked *poco a poco accelerando* or *ritardando*.

---

[8]One should note the difference between *ritardando* (present participle) and *ritenuto* (perfect participle). One means "slowing don," the other, "held back." The latter actually calls for a sudden change of tempo.

There are also instances of composed *ritardandi* in which a succession of notes of smaller time value is followed by notes of increasingly longer duration.

Example 56: Brahms, *Rhapsody in G Minor, Op. 79, No. 2*

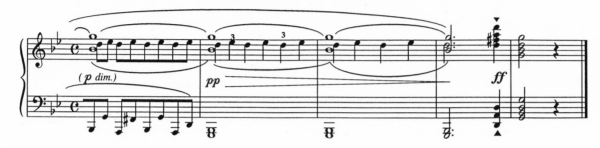

The opposite occurs in the case of composed *accelerandi*. In each case the beat must remain steady; otherwise the effect intended by the composer is nullified.

Sometimes a performer initiates an *accelerando* while holding a longer note. The effect, however, leaves the listener with the impression that the note was not held long enough.

Example 57:

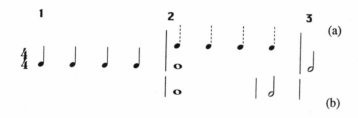

(a) This is what the listener expects, since pulse and meter are clearly established.

(b) This is what the listener hears if the performer fails to keep track of the underlying beat (the downbeat of bar 3 comes too early).

Jumping the gun, as in the above example, can easily be avoided if the performer makes it a rule to keep aware of the basic pulse and all its subdivisions.

RUBATO

The other kind of deviation from a steady beat is usually identified by the term *rubato*.[9] It is not often marked by composers; but one hardly ever hears a performance which unfolds entirely in metronomic fashion and does not contain numerous instances of *rubato*. The specific

---

[9]As defined in the *Harvard Dictionary of Music*, "an elastic flexible tempo involving slight accelerandos and ritardandos that alternate according to the requirements of musical expression."

application of *rubato* depends in large part on the taste and sensitivity of the individual performer. Nevertheless, it is possible to identify some guiding principles which can be of assistance in this delicate area of performance.

"RHYTHMIC ELASTICITY"

First and foremost, **the continuity and flow of the music must never be impaired.** There should be no sudden gaps or jerks. The listener should always be "part of the action," never feel left out, or even out of step. One of the essential requirements toward achieving this is what—for want of a better word—might be called "rhythmic elasticity." In simplest terms, this means that adjoining pulses or subdivisions of a beat must expand or contract "elastically," as is demonstrated in the following graph.

Example 58:

It can readily be seen that the distance between the notes increases and decreases by degrees. One of the attributes of skillfully applied *rubato* is that the identity of beat and meter is never lost, in spite of the tempo fluctuations. **The listener must be able to perceive adjoining identical notes to be of equal value.** Once such equal notes are stretched—or shortened—to the point that they sound like notes of double or half the value, the listener becomes disoriented. In order to avoid any danger of confusion, the performer must take care to keep his tempo adjustments well within safe limits.

Example 59: Chopin, *Impromptu II, Op. 36*

The *rubato* in the first version on the tape (Ex. 59a) is subtle and pleasing. The second version (59b) is deliberately distorted in order to demonstrate what happens when the performer overdoes a good thing. While similar excesses can be avoided easily, they are unfortunately not uncommon.

An awareness of the elements of "rhythmic elasticity" described here will help the performer achieve flexibility while avoiding the kind of excessive capriciousness which may leave the listener bewildered.

Historically, *tempo rubato* began as a rhythmic shift above a constant, even bass, as illustrated and explained below.

Example 60: Türk, *Klavierschule, 1789*

"*Tempo rubato* . . . signifies a stolen, or robbed time, the application of which is . . . left to the judgement of the performer. These words . . . commonly . . . signify a manner of shortening, and lengthening notes; that is to say, a part is taken from the length of one note and given to the other . . . by an anticipation or by a retardation" (cited in Donington, *The Interpretation of Early Music*).

By and large, this kind of *rubato* has been superseded by one in which the changes of tempo affect the entire texture.

To try and set up strict rules concerning the use and degree of *rubato* would seem to limit the subtleties and the flexibility which make *rubato* the wonderful artistic tool it is. Nevertheless, it is possible to make some additional observations concerning its nature and occurrence:

1.   A hesitation is most frequently followed by a compensating acceleration, and vice versa.[10]

Example 61: Chopin, *Nocturne in C Minor, Op. 48, No. 1*

---

[10]The wavy line (～∨＼⟶) indicates a hesitation, the straight line with arrow an acceleration and, most often, a return to the prevailing tempo.

2.   Such hesitation or broadening is most often found on the first, the "strong," beat of a measure, or the focal point of a phrase or passage.

Example 62:   Chopin, *Prelude in E Minor, Op. 28, No. 4*

3.   Pick-up groups of several shorter notes leading to a heavily accented downbeat note of longer time value are often combined with an *allargando*. When the downbeat is slightly withheld or lengthened, as part of such a *rubato*, the effect is identical with that of an agogic accent.[11]

Example 63:   Brahms, *Intermezzo, Op. 118, No. 2*

4.   Sometimes an *appoggiatura* seems to call for a *rubato*-like hesitation.

Example 64a: Schubert, *Piano Sonata in A Major, Op. 120*, Andante

---

[11]See Chapter Six.

The restrained nature of this movement allows only a slight *rubato* (Ex. 23a on the tape). Without it, however, the piece would sound quite inane (23b).

5.   In the following passage the three *forte* notes are usually taken slightly slower. Not only does this sound more convincing, it also helps to alert the listener to the introduction of the coming new musical idea. Depending on the context, which must always be considered first, similar sudden dynamic changes may call for some degree of *rubato*.

Example 65: Beethoven, *Symphony No. 6 in F Major, Op. 68*, 1st Movement

6.   *Rubato* is a delicate device.[12] It is easy to overdo it. One can guard against this in part by avoiding successive and frequent repetitions of identical *rubato* patterns. One must also avoid treating *rubato* in such a way that equal notes, a series of eighths or sixteenths, e.g., are simply played unevenly, without regard to the overall flow.

Example 66: Beethoven, *Piano Sonata in C Minor, Op. 13, Pathétique*, 2nd Movement

---

[12]Chopin once illustrated *rubato* to a pupil. First he blew gently upon a candle in front of him and, making it flicker, remarked: "See, that is *my rubato*;" he then blew the candle out, adding, "and that is *your rubato*." (Quoted in Tobias Matthay, *Musical Interpretation*, p. 79)

When the notes with asterisks are shortened indiscriminately, the effect is a bit like someone limping or lurching.

FUNCTION OF *RUBATO* IN DEFINING STRUCTURE

Certain fluctuations of tempo play an important role in defining musical structure. They have the function of introducing or marking the repeat of material heard before, as, for example, the recapitulation in a sonata form. Most often they will consist of retards too subtle to carry the indication *ritardando*. Sometimes there will be an acceleration toward the new section when the immediately preceding section has been slower than the prevailing tempo. Handled properly, these tempo fluctuations are not only helpful in defining the form and message of the music, but the effect in itself is delightful.

Minuets and scherzos of the classic period are usually followed by their trios without any indication in the score of any pause or tempo change whatever; but these often do make the performance more interesting and attractive and may be justified on the following counts:

1. Any time the texture of the trio is substantially different from that of the minuet or scherzo, a tempo adjustment may be called for, usually toward a slower pace. The kind of experimentation suggested throughout this chapter will again lead to a satisfactory choice.

Example 67: Haydn, *Symphony No. 94 in G Major, Surprise,* Menuetto

In this example the beginning of the movement is included to establish the brisk tempo of the Menuetto, in contrast to the amiable and appropriately slower Trio.

2. A short *Luftpause* between main movement and trio and again at the *da capo* will help set off these sections. If in doubt, one can try and connect them, if only to make sure that a hesitation and/or change of pace are really preferable.

Example 68: Mozart, *Symphony No. 36 in C Major, K. 425, Linz,* Menuetto

54

The following illustrations from the Symphony No. 3 by Brahms admirably exemplify the need for subtle *rubato*-like fluctuations of tempo. None of them are marked by the composer and some of the passages are often performed at a steady pace, without *rubato*. Yet when one juxtaposes versions with and without *rubato*, those with *rubato* seem incomparably more satisfying. Sometimes the need for such tempo adjustments will be suggested by a change in texture, sometimes by the beginning of a new section. The passages cited here are only samples of the kind of musical contexts which allow—or call for—such nuances of pacing. They are also excellent illustrations of subtle tempo changes which, applied with discretion and sensitivity, enhance a performance immeasurably.

Example 69:   Brahms, *Symphony No. 3 in F Major, Op. 90*, 1st Movement

Example 70: Brahms, *Symphony No. 3 in F Major, Op. 90*, 1st Movement

Each style period—even each composer—may require a different approach with regard to tempo fluctuations. Music of the classic period, as the term "classic" suggests, should generally be treated with restraint, while that of the romantic period obviously allows more freedom and abandon.

One must add that pieces, particularly for solo instruments, which are based on one running motive only and have the same figuration throughout, almost invariably call for *rubato.*

Example 71: Schumann, *Arabesque*

Nevertheless there are also certain compositions, especially toccatas, etudes, and the kinds of pieces called *perpetuum mobile*, in which a constant speed is maintained throughout.

It cannot be stressed enough that even a performer quite sure of his instinct will, in dealing with *rubato* and the like, greatly add to his judgment and security through careful analysis and some calculated experimentation.

FERMATAS AND OTHER PAUSES

A discussion of fermatas and other pauses is included here, since they, too, constitute tempo adjustments, though their relation to the prevailing beat is usually not obvious. While the treatment of fermatas depends mainly on the performer's discretion, some guidelines may be in order.

1. The time value of a note with a fermata must be longer than it is without it. This seems obvious; but many recordings prove that this suggestion is not unnecessary. The performer will do well to count the beats of the written note and its subdivisions, particularly when longer time values or slow tempos are involved. The same caution is in order in the case of general pauses. Unless the performer counts throughout the rest and with precision, the following entrance is likely to come too soon.

The exact elongation of the fermata-note can again be determined through experimentation. Once this has been accomplished, one should assign to this elongation a specific number of beats or their subdivisions. (When the adrenalin flows, one's sense of time and tempo is likely to be impaired.)

2.　The same procedure applies to fermatas on the final note of a piece.

3.　Certain fermatas are familiar from their regular use in chorales or anthems. When first introduced centuries ago, these indicated to the congregation where to take a breath—together. In general congregational use these take the value of an extra beat or two. Many present-day conductors ignore them or observe them only when they feel text and punctuation requires some separation.[13]

4.　Some fermatas occur within a phrase. Their proper execution depends not only on the ability of a performer to find a convincing length for the hold, but also to maintain the flow of the phrase in spite of the delay. At times such a hold will be prepared with a *ritardando* and left with a subtle *accelerando*, back to the prevailing tempo. As long as the performer knows the entire range of options and tries them, one by one, he will be able to find the most desirable and appropriate solution.

Example 72:　Massenet, *Manon*, Gavotte

5.　An *allargando* is almost mandatory before the fermatas which indicate the start of a cadenza, especially in concerto movements.

6.　It may be in order to draw attention to other kinds of pauses which interrupt the flow of the music; they are usually indicated thus　//　or　’　and are generally called *Luftpausen* or caesuras, though other colloquial expressions are also used.

In certain contexts *Luftpausen* have to be inserted which are not marked by composers. They are necessary when a *f* is followed by a *p* or *pp subito*.[14] Such short pauses allow the reverberation generated by the preceding *f* to subside and facilitate a clean

---

[13]The rugged simplicity of the tunes thus often gives way to a sophisticated glibness or to an expressive quality which impairs their naive beauty. This, however, is a matter of taste which will not be further pursued here.
[14]See Chapter Two, p. 17.

start for the *p* or *pp* passage. When the *p* is preceded by a sufficiently long note, such a note is simply shortened to allow for a clear separation, without any retardation.

Example 73:   Brahms, *Symphony No. 1 in C Minor, Op. 68*, 4th Movement

Here the need for a substantial pause is even more obvious in view of the change in tempo.

Example 74:   Bartók, *Mikrokosmos, Vol. VI*, Ostinato

Example 75: Beethoven, *Symphony No. 9 in D Minor, Op. 125*, 4th Movement

In bar 32 all the strings have a rest on the fourth quarter. The *staccato* dots in the wind parts suggest a similar rest, thus a *Luftpause* of the kind discussed. Accordingly, the second half note in the vocal parts must similarly be shortened for the sake of clarity and conformity, adding to the magic of the ensuing *piano subito*.

Chapter Five

ARTICULATION

THE TERM "ARTICULATION"

According to the dictionary "to articulate" means "to utter distinctly." With regard to speech articulation also refers to the enunciation of consonants and vowels as well as to their connection and separation in the process of forming words.

As for music, the term "articulation" is used "to denote clarity and distinct rendition in performance."[1] It also refers to the connection and separation of individual notes.

LEGATO

The connection of notes (*legato*) seems simple enough: one note is held right up to the next. The voice and certain instruments[2] lend themselves readily to the execution of a true *legato*. The following example can be sung easily without break, on one vowel or one syllable. It can be played equally smoothly on any wind or bowed string instrument, on one breath, and on one bow, respectively.

Example 76:

On non-sustaining instruments, however, such as the piano, the harp, guitar and others, the *legato* requires special treatment. Each tone has its decay pattern, i.e., the amplitude of the vibration—and with it the volume—diminishes immediately and at a built-in rate, beyond the performer's control. In the case of the piano merely holding down one key until the next is depressed does not in itself produce a satisfactory *legato*, particularly if each note is attacked with equal force.[3]

---

[1]Quoted from the *Harvard Dictionary of Music.*
[2]In terms of articulation the division of instruments into sustaining and non-sustaining categories is much more useful than their classification according to material and manner of sound generation.
[3]The damper pedal of the piano and certain devices on some percussion instruments will not be discussed here, even though their skillful use can enhance the impression of *legato* in some circumstances.

Example 77:

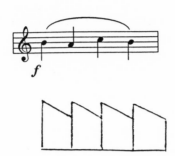

The slanted lines represent the "decay," the automatic reduction in volume. The volume indications (the vertical lines) do not represent exact dynamic values, but only an approximation of the relative volume of each note.

On non-sustaining instruments a reasonably effective *legato* is achieved by adjusting the volume of a note to that of the preceding note at the moment of articulation, thus:

Example 78:

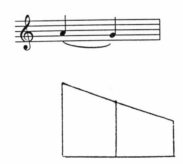

One would logically conclude that applying this approach to a group of notes produces a continuous *diminuendo*, resulting in total silence in short order. In actual practice, however, the performer makes continuous subtle dynamic adjustments which effectively simulate *legato*, and in *crescendo* as well. What is essential here is to maintain the distinction between accented and unaccented notes. The following examples illustrate a number of configurations in which *legato* is simulated.

Example 79: Two-note groups

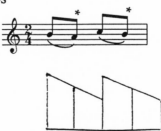

In this and the following examples each second eighth note (marked by an asterisk *) is made slightly softer than the preceding quarter.

Example 80: Descending four-note groups

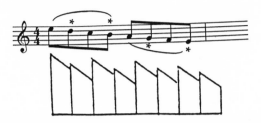

Here the volume is adjusted to avoid an excessive *descrescendo*.

Example 81: *Crescendo*

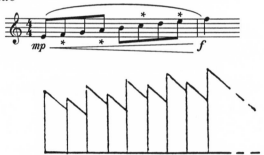

In this figure the notes falling on the quarter beats carry the *crescendo*, with "1" and "3" retaining their relative emphasis as primary and secondary accents. The intervening unaccented eighth notes are adjusted to avoid a hammered, *non legato* effect.

String players can manage to produce a satisfactory *legato* even when using up-and-down bowing, provided all bowing accents and any kind of separation are avoided.[4]

THE MANY DEGREES OF SEPARATION

While there is essentially only one kind of *legato*—the notes simply are connected—there are many degrees of separation, from the shortest *staccato* to a barely noticeable separation of notes. The articulation marks and the designations commonly used are indicated below:

---

[4]Theodore Salzman, for years the principal cellist of the Pittsburgh Symphony, had an "endless," seamless *legato*. One had to watch him to know that his bow changed direction; one could not hear it. Asked about the secret of his teaching magic, when one of his Congress of Strings students displayed the same technique after only two weeks of lessons, he answered, "I don't let them play a phrase until they sing it to perfection."

Example 82:

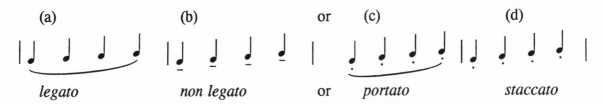

(a) (b) or (c) (d)

legato *non legato* or *portato* *staccato*

To apply a rule of thumb, in the case of *portato* or non *legato* the notes may be held from about half to almost the full value of the written note, as long as the separation remains distinct. A *staccato* note may have an actual duration of one-fourth to one-half the value of the written note (in the case of a quarter, thus: ♪ to ♪), although it may frequently be even shorter.[5]

Concerning the length of *staccato* notes the statement of C. P. E. Bach still has validity: "One must make a distinction in *staccato*, and take into account the value of the note, whether the tempo be swift or slow, whether the dynamic sense is *forte* or *piano*; these notes are always held for somewhat less than half their value. In general, it can be said that *staccato* takes place mostly with leaps and in fast tempo."[6]

In the absence of articulation marks (slurs and *staccato* dots, or their combination, and others) the intervals of a melodic line may suggest the appropriate articulation: ". . . especially in older music . . . the most natural articulation is to bind together in *legato* the intervals of seconds, to separate slightly the notes of the middle-sized intervals by means of *portato*, and to separate distinctly the large intervals (those that we commonly designate as 'leaps')."[7]

There is a tendency among some performers, however, to treat all *staccato* notes the same, so that little or no difference is made between *staccato* half notes, quarter notes, or eighths, etc. But **if the composer took the trouble to indicate these differences, the performer should take note of them and adjust the length of the actual sound accordingly**. Above all it is the mood or character of a passage which determines the duration of the *staccato* notes and, correspondingly, the length of the gap between sounds.

There are times when a composer will indicate articulation patterns that go against these otherwise useful and simple guidelines, as in the following example:

Example 83: Beethoven, *Piano Trio in E Flat Major, Op. 1, No. 1*, 4th Movement

---

[5]Concerning the use of the wedge ( ) to indicate a very short *staccato*, see Hermann Keller, *Phrasing and Articulation*, p. 47 ff.

[6]Hermann Keller, *op. cit.*, p. 55 ff.

[7]Hermann Keller, *op. cit.*, p. 36.

INTERPRETING SLURS

The last note of a slurred group is generally shortened, as a matter of course, separating it from the following group.[8]

Example 84: Beethoven, *Bagatelle, Op. 119, No. 1*

Quite frequently slurs are routinely marked to fit within a measure, or to conform to each beat, merely with the purpose of indicating *legato* in general (Ex. 85). In such cases the slurred groups must not be separated, in contrast to Ex. 86, where the slurs do signify the boundaries of adjoining but distinctly separate groupings.

Example 85: Beethoven, *Sonata in D Major for Piano Duet, Op. 6,* Rondo

Example 86: Brahms, *Intermezzo, Op. 119, No. 2*

---

[8]See also Chapter Six.

GROUPS FORMED THROUGH ARTICULATION

In reading a text the shift of commas or other punctuation marks often results in a change of meaning. Similarly, changes in articulation bring about changes in the character of a passage, even though the notes themselves remain the same.

Example 87:

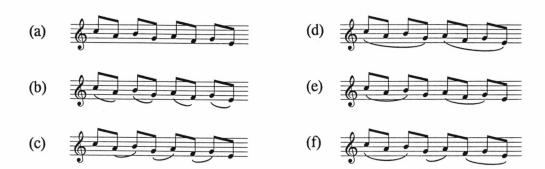

Hermann Keller refers to this phenomenon, illustrated here in its simplest form, as "formation of groups through articulation" (in the original German *Gruppenbildung durch Artikulation*).[9]

This very useful concept points up the broad effect articulation in its many ramifications has on interpretation. The performer who learns to regard articulation as a means of expression rather than a mere technical device (as, e.g., in the case of bowing and tonguing techniques perfunctorily applied) invariably adds to the interest and impact of his performance.

Among the many elements affecting articulation one should be mentioned yet, that of non-harmonic tones. In general these are resolved stepwise up or down, as in the case of *appoggiaturas*, e.g.

Example 88:   Appoggiaturas

It happens only rarely that the resolution is separated from the non-harmonic tone, and usually only for a special characteristic effect.[10]

---

[9]See Keller, *op. cit.*, p. 53.
[10]See Example 109.

Example 89:

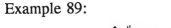

While these two figures appear similar, there is this difference: in the first the long note is followed by one of the same pitch. This re-articulation also results in a separation and, depending on the context, may allow for a slight phrase accent to mark the beginning of the next phrase.[11] In the second, the long note is followed by a non-harmonic note—a passing tone—which should normally be slurred to the preceding long note. For that reason, and also because it falls on the second eighth note of the group, it should not receive an accent.

The following passage provides illustrations for both separation and connection, as described above.

Example 90: J. S. Bach, *The Well-Tempered Clavier, Vol. II,* Prelude in E Major

VARIETIES OF ARTICULATION

With regard to speech the term "articulation" may be said to apply to different kinds of delivery, from crisp to drawling, from booming to whispering. In music, too, the effect of articulation goes far beyond the mere connection and separation of notes, and in its various aspects determines to a remarkable degree the character of a performance. The elements involved are, in addition to the actual durational value of the notes, their dynamic level and shape, and the very quality of the attack, which in the case of certain instruments greatly affects their timbre. The performer intent on bringing a piece of music to life in all its variety and detail thus will not be satisfied with mere "clarity" and "a distinct rendition."

There are numerous terms denoting varieties of articulation. Some of them apply only to certain instruments, especially those referring to the bowing styles of string instruments; but their effect can often be imitated or simulated on other instruments.[12] In any case, they convey a wide spectrum of possible articulation, in terms of volume as well as timbre, suggesting both the duration of the tone and the quality of the attack.

---

[11]See p. 96.
[12]See Vladimir Ashkenazy's statement quoted in Chapter Nine, p. 132.

List of terms denoting varieties of articulation:

marcato	Bowing styles:
martellato	*détaché*
staccato	*spiccato*
staccatissimo	*saltando*
non legato	flying *staccato*
portato	flying *spiccato*
leggiero	*ricochet*
leggierissimo	

In addition, such terms as *con forza, ruvido*, (rough, harsh), *carezzando* (caressing), *piacevole* (agreeable, charming), and the like are used to suggest modes of articulation.

ATTACK AND RELEASE

In shaping individual notes the quality of the release is almost as important as the quality of the attack. Singers in particular, who may begin a tone gently and beautifully, often neglect to end it in similar fashion, stopping abruptly. The graphs below illustrate the desirable dynamic shape as well as the less satisfactory, sudden cutoff.

Example 91:

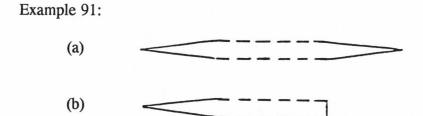

(a)

(b)

Once a performer has become aware of this phenomenon, he will find it relatively easy to control the length and quality of the decay. In general the release should match the attack.

Many performers pay little attention to the time value of the last note of the group prior to a rest. Thus ♩♩‑ | may inadvertently be turned into ♩♩ ↓ | or even ♩♪ ↓ |. Obviously the note in question should be sustained right up to the following beat (in our example up to the third quarter).[13]

When different kinds of articulation are used simultaneously—in chamber music or in larger ensembles—problems of balance and coordination arise. In most cases the approach of the various members of an ensemble will differ enough to necessitate adjustments beyond simply minding the dynamic and articulation signs in the score. Most composers will have considered the idiosyncrasies of the instruments themselves and the relative effect of various kinds of articulation and marked the parts accordingly; but only if the performers carefully monitor the sounds actually produced can the proper ensemble be achieved.

There are instances in which distinct articulation is not desirable; for example, when *tremolo* in strings or winds is to produce a throbbing or shimmering effect rather than a rhythmically defined pattern. This also applies in piano music, particularly in the case of transcriptions from orchestral music when *tremolo* effects are imitated. By comparison, passages such as the following are meant to be played as written, with each note clearly articulated.

---

[13]A note of caution concerning final consonants in vocal music: as shown in the example below, they should be placed just before the end of the note in order to keep the following rest completely free. Especially in the case of voiced consonants which have an audible pitch (in this example the encircled m), a harmonic clash may otherwise result.

Example 92: Lassus, Motet *"Adoramus te Christe"*

Example 93: Mozart, *Fantasia in C Minor, K.475*

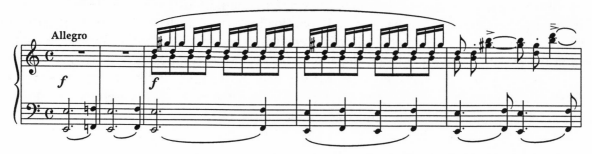

A note about *pizzicato* may be in order here. Its tone quality varies greatly from player to player, from string to string on the same instrument, and even from high to low on the same string. A little sensitivity with respect to the quality of sounds can make a great deal of difference. If the individual performer can think of emulating the tone quality produced by fine harp and guitar players, the improvement is immediate and striking.

From time to time methods of articulation are routinely applied which do not arise from the musical context. One example is the indiscriminate brilliant and energetic off-the-string playing favored by many violinists, which does not fit every style. Other examples of idiosyncrasies, especially among string players, are (1) articulation accents and (2) change-of-bow swells. The articulation accents are little dynamic "swells" in *legato* phrases like the following:[14]

Example 94: Beethoven, *Violin Sonata in C Minor, Op. 30, No. 2*, 2nd Movement

This introduces an element of fussiness into an otherwise tranquil context (Ex. 94a on the tape). As for the "change-of-bow swells," which happen immediately before the bow changes directions, they interfere with the continuity and flow of extended lines. These and other routinely applied methods of articulation—not arising from the context—are likely to draw attention to themselves rather than illuminating the musical idea.

SHAPES OF LONGER NOTES

In determining the dynamic shape of notes it is again helpful to turn to language. It is a simple but important fact of speech that every syllable is beginning-accented, i.e., it is loudest at the start and gets softer immediately. In normal speech this happens so fast that one generally

---

[14]There are two versions of Example 94 on the tape, the second without the swells described above (94b).

is not aware of the phenomenon itself. When words are set to music, however, speech is slowed and syllables are elongated. In shaping the notes—according to the normal tendency of speech just described—it is necessary to keep the syllables, and with them the notes, beginning-accented. One can, however, hear a good many singers starting each longer note softly, then letting it "balloon." This process, indiscriminately applied, sounds artificial and impairs the flow of a phrase. The two taped versions of the following example illustrate these approaches, one of them being notably more satisfactory (95b).

Example 95: Hageman, Do Not Go, My Love

Do   not   go,   my love,   with-out ask-ing my leave.

String and wind players, too, can be heard to indulge in ballooning, a habit anyone can easily fall into, unless he keeps aware of the larger aspects of the musical structure.

In this context one should mention a rather common occurrence: many string players can be heard to play the figure ♩. ♩ in such a way that the quarter note is louder than the dotted half note. Since the bow travels three times faster (on the ♩), the bow pressure must be reduced accordingly. If the player has the appropriate sounds in mind, the problem disappears; if not, the two notes will sound like someone saying "darLING" (♩. ♩) instead of "DARling."

Long notes are rarely sustained on one unchanging dynamic level.[15] Most often there will be a rise and a corresponding drop in volume, thus:

Example 96:   O

If one listens to performances of fine artists, one will hear that the usual dynamic shape will approximate that shown in the following graph, similar to a parabolic curve:

---

[15]Except on the organ and on certain electronic instruments, as well as recent music in which such effects are imitated on conventional instruments.

Example 97:

In other words, the rise is slow, the drop faster. But the most satisfactory shape is one in which there is an initial, somewhat louder attack, followed first by a short slight *decrescendo* and then the *crescendo-decrescendo* pattern described above. This also satisfies the obvious requirement that even in *pp* the attack must be above the threshold of audibility.

One of the most common problems of articulation has to do with the nature of the voice and certain sustaining instruments. Any time a performer has to hold a long note, he will need to save breath or bow. As a result, he may start the note with a limited amount of volume or energy. Example 98 illustrates what happens in this case, i.e., when, in a *forte* context, the long note begins *p* instead of *f*.

Example 98:

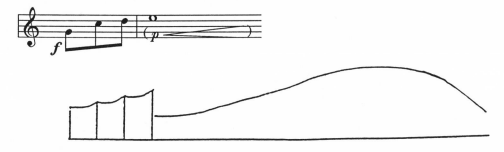

Example 99:

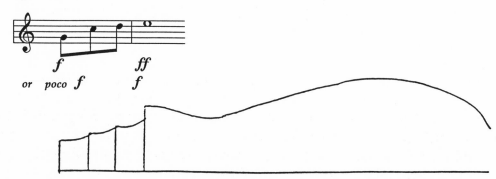

The graph in Example 99 represents the "most satisfactory" note shape described above, with the downbeat louder than the pick-up notes.

The following familiar excerpt provides an excellent illustration of the kinds of beginning-accented long notes discussed above.

Example 100: Handel, *Messiah*, I Know that My Redeemer Liveth

and that He   shall stand——— at the lat - - - ter— day————— up on the earth.

SYNCOPATION

The dynamic shape of syncopated notes—on the **off**-beat—is essentially the same as that of notes **on** the beat; in other words, they are **beginning-accented**.

Example 101:

(a)   **On** the beat

(b)   Syncopation

The following scheme negates the proper effect of the syncopation and should be avoided.

Example 102:

It must be kept in mind that **a syncopation is only perceived as such if there is an awareness of the underlying metric scheme**. Sometimes the written syncopations take the place of regular metric accents. In that case a metric shift has actually taken place, even if for the sake of convenience the composer has retained the barring scheme.

In playing syncopations like the following, the performer must make sure that the tied note on "1" does not disappear and is still heard, in spite of the *decrescendo*.

Example 103:

Similarly, when the pick-up group of triplets in Example 104 is played too vigorously and the downbeat note is very short and does not receive the proper emphasis, the listener can easily misconstrue the pattern and its metric orientation (as indicated by the broken barlines and the accent signs $\mid \cup$).

Example 104: Haydn, *String Quartet, Op. 76, No. 1*, 4th Movement

Conductor Robert Shaw at one time told of a conversation he had with Alexander Schneider during a stroll on the beaches of Puerto Rico. It was when he had his first encounter with Pablo Casals, quite overwhelmed at the force and magic of his artistry. When he asked what in Schneider's opinion was the secret of that artistry, the answer was "the way he goes from one note to the next."

There is some significance in the fact that Isaac Stern, when asked (by Dick Cavett) what sets a great violinist apart from any other competent fiddler, also said "the way he goes from one note to the next."

This means, of course, the manner of separation and connection of notes, of their attack and shape—in other words—of articulation in all its ramifications.

Chapter Six

ACCENTS

In this book the term "accent" is applied to a tone which stands out among others.[1]

FUNCTION AND GENERAL CATEGORIES OF ACCENTS

One basic function of accents, which is to define rhythmic groupings—similar to the function of syllabic and syntactic accents in speech—has been discussed before.[2] In this chapter we shall be concerned with (1) accents which do not necessarily arise from the musical context but are marked by composers in order to assure that the characteristic and often capricious quality of a musical idea is brought out in performance; (2) a large category of accents which generally are not marked which, however, are inherent in the musical structure, and without which a performance sounds unconvincing and inane.

Composers over the centuries have used many symbols to indicate accents. They have not always agreed or been individually consistent in their application. Generally, however, the signs and symbols encountered will include

$$\Lambda \, , \, > \, , \, - \quad \text{and } \textit{sfz, fz, sf, rf, rinf., fp.}[3]$$

FACTORS DETERMINING THE LEVELS OF ACCENTS

The specific dynamic values will always depend on the context. For example, *sforzato* in a *piano* passage will be the equivalent of *mp* or *mf*, while in a *forte* or *fortissimo* context it will be more like *ff*, respectively, *fff*. In addition, the style and period of a work, as well as the specific instrument and the range involved, will determine the relative dynamic level of an accent.

Example 105: Haydn, *Piano Sonata in E Flat Major*, 2nd Movement

---

[1] In general parlance the words "stress" and "accent" are interchangeable. I have refrained from assigning to the word "stress" a special meaning in order to avoid ambiguities and misunderstandings.

[2] See Chapter Three.

[3] The terms *sforzato, sforzando (sf, sfz), forzato, forzando (fz)*, and *rinforzando (rf, rfz, rinf.)* and their abbreviations are practically synonymous and all denote sudden accents.

The rather charming accents in bar 3 occur on the weak parts of the second and third beats. If played *mp*—or at the most *mf*—they will have the intended effect.

Example 106: Beethoven, *Piano Sonata in C Minor, Op. 111*, 1st Movement

Since the prevailing dynamic level here is *ff* , the *sf* must be louder, thus *fff* .

ADJUSTING ACCENTS FOR BALANCE AND TRANSPARENCY

The following score excerpt has the identical accents marked from top to bottom. The distribution of pitches proves that Beethoven was very much aware of the relative power of the instruments in their respective ranges. But like other composers of the period he did not differentiate further and expected the performers to adjust the dynamic level of the individual tones in order to achieve balance and transparency.[4]

---

[4]See also footnotes on pp. 7 and 22.

Example 107: Beethoven, *Symphony No. 7 in A Major, Op. 92*, 4th Movement

Example 107a has dynamic marks adjusted in keeping with the normal responses of routined players.

Example 107a:

USING NUMERALS FOR FINER GRADATIONS[5]

In the following example numeric values along a scale from 1 to 20 are assigned to a succession of accents to illustrate their function in achieving the desired dynamic contour. The many signs of > obviously are not intended to mean accents of equal weight.

---

[5]See Chapter Two, p. 15.

On the tape Ex. 108 is given in two versions. The first (108a) is played slowly in order to make it easier to keep track of the subtle gradations of volume.

Example 108: Schumann, *Kreisleriana,* 1st Movement

TYPES OF ACCENTS

Whether a composer marked an accent or not, a particular note or chord will stand out from the context for a number of reasons. Accordingly, various types of accents may be distinguished:

1.	dynamic	6.	texture
2.	agogic[6]	7.	embellishment
3.	metric	8.	color
4.	harmonic	9.	phrase
5.	pitch		

1.   Dynamic Accents:

As the term is used here, these are generally marked by the composer. They do not necessarily arise from the context, but in most cases give the musical ideas in which they occur their characteristic quality. The following illustrations are examples of such accents:

---

[6]Agogics (from the German term *Agogik* and adapted from the original Greek) refers to modifications of tempo, as dynamics refers to gradations of intensity or volume. An agogic accent therefore involves the lengthening of notes.

Example 109: Beethoven, *Violin Sonata in D Major, Op. 12, No. 1*, 3rd Movement

Example 110: Beethoven, *Bagatelle, Op. 33, No. 2*

Without these accents the phrases in question lose their special capricious character and sound weak and colorless (Example 110a on the tape).

In addition to the ever-present challenge to find an appropriate level for each dynamic accent, the following points should be kept in mind:

a.   An accented note of any length will divide into two parts: the louder, accented part, and that part in which the volume of the note returns to the prevailing level. This principle applies to sustaining instruments, not to the piano or to plucked and most percussion instruments whose tones, once sounded, fade away.

b.   In each case the durational value of the accent has to be determined. A *fp* on a whole note may typically be divided thus:

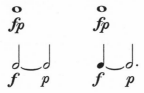

Accents marked with the signs ∧ , > , or *sf*, etc., will have to be treated similarly. In each case an analysis of the context and some experimentation will produce

80

an appropriate solution. In ensemble music especially, coordination of this sort is essential and should be carefully planned by the conductor or leader.

The following examples serve to illustrate accents whose duration ranges from the shortest possible impact[7] to almost the entire length of the note in question.

Example 111: Brahms, *Symphony No. 1 in C Minor, Op. 68*, 4th Movement

---

[7]This is sometimes called an "acute" accent, while to its opposite the designation "leaning" accent may be applied.

The heavy *staccato* chord at bar 183 of Example 111 has *fp* marked in the violas and the bassoons. If the bassoons' *fp* is to correspond to that of the violas (), their whole note will have to be divided thus:

Example 112: Beethoven, *Symphony No. 2 in D Major, Op. 36*, 3rd Movement

In view of the fast pace of the movement, the *fp* in bars 22 and 23 of Example 112 may well be broken up in this fashion:

Example 113: Mozart, *Symphony No. 35 in D Major, K. 385*, 2nd Movement

In this example the *p* in the strings in bar 5 determines how the *sfp* in the winds is to be treated: . Having the woodwinds play *p* immediately after an acute accent (*sf*) would take away from the solidity and strength of the chord.

Often a longer note begins with an accent, but has a *decrescendo* (or ⎯⎯⎯) marked in addition.

Example 114: Beethoven, *Symphony No. 4 in B Flat Major, Op. 60*, 3rd Movement

Prolonged "leaning" accents, as in Ex. 115, often begin with special force, the equivalent of "acute" accents, thus: ♩♪ or ♪♩ .

Example 115: Beethoven, *Symphony No. 3 in E Flat Major, Op. 55*, 1st Movement

2.   Agogic Accents:

Strictly speaking, any longer note will draw attention to itself by virtue of its duration and thus represents an agogic accent.

Example 116:   Chopin, *Scherzo in B Flat Minor, Op. 31*

In this context, however, we will deal with those agogic accents (marked ↓) which involve a deviation from the metronomic pulse.   Of these there are two kinds:

a.   A withholding of the stressed beat (most often the downbeat, the "strong" beat of a measure or group), and

b.   A lengthening of the accented note.

Agogic accents of the first kind are typically found where the accented note or chord is preceded by a large skip or a group of notes unmanageable or incongruous at regular speed.   In some passages a climactic impact or explosion is approached with a "windup," which may be compared to an athlete's running approach to a high or broad jump.   (A very funny visualization of the wrong approach, defying the law of gravity, is familiar from the *Roadrunner* cartoons.)

Example 117:   Rachmaninoff, *Prelude, Op. 32, No. 12*

Example 118: Chopin, *Ballade in A Flat Major, Op. 47*

Bars 235 and 236 in this example have the *arpeggio* begin on the beat, with definite time values assigned to the notes. This conclusively emphasizes the difference in the execution of bars 231 and 233, on one hand, and bars 235 and 236, on the other. As in Example 117, the grace notes require more time than a metronomic rendition permits. This results in an agogic accent, i.e., a slight delay of the downbeat.

Sometimes the impact of a note or chord, lacking such a windup, is simply delayed for the dramatic effect desired.

Example 119: Brahms, *Rhapsody in G Minor, Op. 79, No. 2*

In this example the two forceful chords stand out from the surrounding triplet pattern. That fact, and the composer's indication *risoluto* as well as the wedge (▾) and accent signs (＞) suggest a separation between the first and second beats of each measure in question. A slight delay of the second beat enhances the effect.

The second type of agogic accent is used a great deal, often in combination with dynamic emphasis. The specific elongation of the accented note and the deviation from the regular pulse invariably arise from the context. (Some performers prefer to avoid or minimize such agogic accents.)

Example 120: Chopin, *Etude in A Flat Major, Op. 25, No. 1*

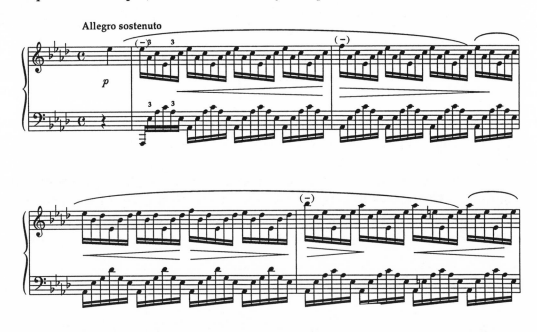

This kind of accent is often preceded by an *allargando* and followed by a corresponding *accelerando*, back to the prevailing tempo. When a number of such agogic accents, with their incidental tempo adjustments, follow in succession, the effect is similar to *rubato*.[8]

---

[8]See Chapter Cour, p. 48 ff.

Example 121: Liszt, *Piano Sonata*

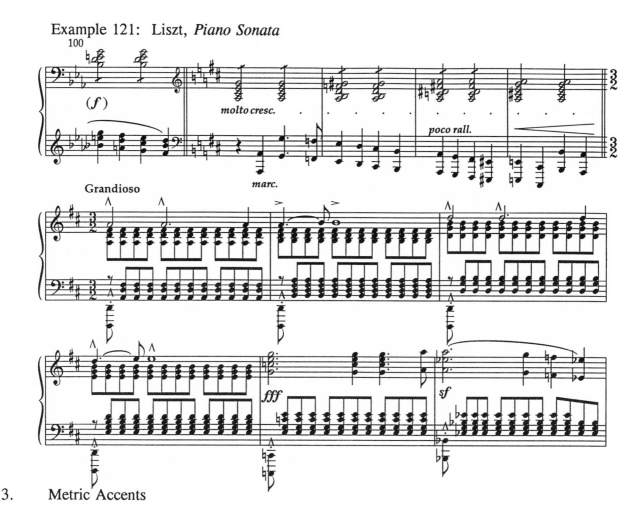

3. Metric Accents

Every metric group has its metric accent on the first, the "strong" or "down"-beat. In the following example the quarter rest of the repeated motive and the pitch accent (see below) combine in putting special emphasis on each downbeat. As has been pointed out, however, repeated stereotyped downbeat accents tend to sound objectionable.

Example 122: Beethoven, *Piano Sonata in E Flat Major, Op. 31, No. 3*, 1st Movement

More often than not, a metric accent is barely noticeable in a "musical" performance in which regular downbeat accents are avoided. When two or more measures combine to form a "large" measure (*Grosstakt*),[9] only one of the downbeats will be noticeably emphasized.

The following excerpt is a famous example notable for the fact that Beethoven himself marked the passage *ritmo di tre battute* and *quattro battute* (rhythm of three, respectively, four beats).

Example 123: Beethoven, *Symphony No. 9 in D Minor, Op. 125*, 2nd Movement

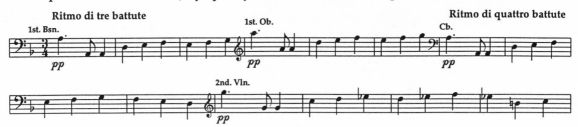

Sometimes syncopations or off-beat accents are so pronounced that the meter easily becomes obscured.

Example 124: Schubert, *Moments Musicaux, Op. 94, No. 4*

Example 125: Beethoven, *String Quartet in E Minor, Op. 59, No. 2*, 3rd Movement

---

[9]See also Chapter Three, p. 32.

The graceful effect of the Schubert example (124a on the tape) and the delicious rhythmic teaser in Example 125 give way to clumsiness and discomfort when the correct rhythmic orientation is lost (124b). In other words, a metric emphasis—on the downbeat—must be maintained on a minimal dynamic level.

Some phrases which at first glance appear quite regular do not coincide with the barring. The restatement of the theme in the following example begins in the middle of bar 5.

Example 126: J. S. Bach, *Brandenburg Concerto No. 6 in B Flat Major*, 1st Movement

In this case the musical idea retains its rhythmic identity and the appropriate accents. To the ear of the listener it is unmistakably the same, but it appears in the "wrong" place on the printed page. It is helpful, even essential, to recognize this deviation in order to avoid misleading metric accents (on each "downbeat").

Example 127: Hindemith, *Piano Duet*, 2nd Movement

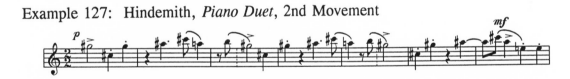

In many similar cases, as in the above example, the regular barring scheme is simply retained for the sake of convenience in reading and performance.[10]

4.   Harmonic Accents:

The traditional concepts of dissonance and consonance, and with them tension and relaxation, may be translated here into terms of relative weight and, therefore,

---

[10]In his book *The Composer's Advocate*, Erich Leinsdorf says: "First we have to look at the meaning of bar lines in general. They are a musical version of the grid on a map. When we walk in nature, there are no lines of longitude and latitude criss-crossing the ground. Such markings are for plotting and survey but not for the enjoyment of nature. It is the same with bar lines; they are our grid, convenient for the mechanical progress of rehearsal and performance, but they must never intrude on the hearer's consciousness, unless of course there is a special reason in rhythmic design . . ." (p. 139) See also Chapter Three, p. 35.

dynamic inflections. It is useful to quote here from Quantz[11], who recognized that chromatic alterations and dissonant chords required some dynamic emphasis, and therefore arrived at this rather quaint and extreme-looking scheme:

Example 128:   Quantz, *Versuch einer Anweisung die Flöte traversiere zu spielen,* Appendix, Ex. XXIV

The concepts involved here may quite properly be applied to harmonic progressions in general, the degree of dissonance calling for corresponding degrees of accentuation (i.e., volume).

Example 129: Schubert, *Piano Sonata in D Major, Op. 53*, 4th Movement

The lovely harmonic surprise, so typical of Schubert, seems to require some dynamic emphasis (>) which would have to be supplied even if there were no *crescendo* indicated.

---

[11]Quantz, Johann Joachim, *On Playing the Flute*, trans. by E. R. Reilly, 2nd ed. (New York: Schirmer Books, 1975)

The following famous quotation exemplifies to perfection the accent produced by strong dissonance, and the succeeding chords represent diminishing degrees of dissonance. The effect is one of relaxation, as if the resolution at the end of the phrase were a consonance and not a dominant 7th chord.

Example 130: Wagner, *Tristan und Isolde,* Prelude

It is, of course, important to remember that the rhythmic and/or metric position of chords will invariably be a potent factor in determining their dynamic weight. Altogether one cannot repeat often enough that **no single principle or factor will dominate, but that the context will determine the relative weight of each component involved.**

5.   Pitch Accents:

A high note will stand out in any context. "High" generally means tension and loudness, "low," relaxation and softness, almost in analogy with the laws of gravity (it takes physical effort to lift things against the pull of gravity).

In a configuration of notes without barring and rhythmization high notes seem to stand out. One automatically assumes that they are louder than low notes. Generally, however, **"meter wins out over pitch."**

Example 131:

In Example 131(a) the encircled note does seem to stand out. In (b) the high note falls on the downbeat, which gives it dynamic emphasis. In (c), however, the metric emphasis is on the note "b," and the high pitch "a," falling on the unaccented second eighth note of the measure, must therefore be softer.

From time to time one hears the following passage as recorded in Example 132a. The dynamic accent on the high pitch then produces a rhythmic dislocation.

91

Example 132: Beethoven, *Piano Sonata in E Major, Op. 109*, 1st Movement

The following examples clearly show that the rhythmic context determines whether "higher" also means "louder." In other words, generally speaking, a pitch accent arises when it coincides with the rhythmic strong point.

Example 133: Beethoven, *Piano Sonata in A Flat Major, Op. 26*, 2nd Movement

Example 134: Beethoven, *Symphony No. 6 in F Major, Op. 68*, 5th Movement

6.   Texture Accents:

This accent simply involves the effect of many tones, or several voices or instruments, coming together in contrast to a single note: one note against a chord, solo quartet, e.g., or against full ensemble or orchestra, etc.

Example 135: Beethoven, *String Quartet in F Major, Op. 18, No. 1*, 1st Movement

Sometimes dynamic emphasis is added; but in the proper context the mere contrast between one or few and many voices—without change of volume—is exactly what the composer intended and the music requires to work its magic.

In the song *Die beiden Grenadiere* a texture accent (off-beat) suggests the limping and lurching of the worn-out French soldiers returning from the Russian front.

Example 136: Schumann, Die beiden Grenadiere

7.   Embellishment Accents:

In the visual arts and in architecture most ornaments by and large are meant to draw attention to themselves and to stand out from the surrounding area. Similarly in music: if properly executed, many ornaments stand out not only by virtue of their melodic and rhythmic attributes, but also due to the fact that they usually involve some dynamic emphasis. Some embellishments begin on the beat and have an accent on the first note, others function as anacruses and end with an accent, also on the beat.

Example 137: J. S. Bach, *Partita No. 4,* Overture

Example 138: Schubert, *Moments Musicaux, Op. 94, No. 3*

Because of the enormous number of symbols and the confusing and often contradictory variety of interpretations a careful study of their use by different composers and different periods is essential.[12]

8.   Color Accents:

The element of color also is a factor in having notes or chords stand out, thus producing the effect of accents. It is the composer, of course, who determines basic

---

[12]For sources concerning ornamentation see the Bibliography.

colors through his instrumentation or, as is the case of Ex. 139, by choosing for certain utterances a particular range. Recognizing the intention of the composer a thoughtful and imaginative performer will be able to discover many subtle variations of sound suitable for color accents and for bringing out the character of a passage.

Example 139: Nicolai, *Die lustigen Weiber von Windsor*, Duet

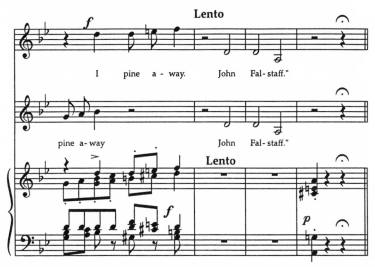

Example 140: Mahler, *Symphony No. 1 in D Major*, 4th Movement

The single (suspended) cymbal stroke (marked *Holz*, i.e., played with a wooden mallet) has to be virtually staggering to make the subsequent overpowering avalanche of sounds believable.

Example 141: St.-Saëns, *Le Carnaval des animaux*, No. 8, Personnages à longues oreilles

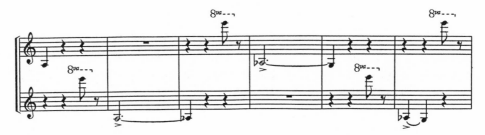

Color contrast can be achieved with mutes, and color accents of various kinds by instruments capable of muting single tones. The French horn, in particular, can produce various gradations of color with different kinds of mutes and stopped and "brassy" tones. Color accents can be achieved on a variety of instruments which have devices or techniques available for such a purpose: varieties of bowing in strings, *vibrato*, *pizzicato*; different mallets in percussion, etc. In other words, the methods used to achieve varieties of color in general can also be used for the enhancement of individual accents.

9.   Phrase Accents:

These are simply dynamic accents used to clarify or emphasize the beginning of a phrase, which in some contexts may easily be covered up. They are especially necessary with certain anacruses, when the tendency of the performer is to start softly in order to allow for a properly unaccent pickup. In the following configurations the lower notes are likely to be lost, especially in low vocal passages:

Example 142:

The dynamic adjustment which the phrase accent provides assures that the notes in question are brought up to a satisfactory level. In the following example such accents invariably prove necessary.

Example 143: Handel, *Messiah,* O Thou That Tellest Good Tidings to Zion

In contrapuntal, imitative passages, even phrase beginnings which occur on a downbeat occasionally have to be emphasized. Again, it is not, strictly speaking, the phrase itself that may require the accent; the phrase beginning simply would be obscured without it.

Example 144: Beethoven, *Symphony No. 7 in A Major, Op. 92,* 1st Movement

When several phrases are joined without rests to separate them, it becomes almost imperative to emphasize the first note of each segment. This use of phrase accents, rather than sounding capricious and out of place, allows the musical structure to emerge and clarifies the segmentation of the text in vocal music.

Example 145: Bach, *English Suite No. 2 in A Minor,* Prelude

Example 146: J. S. Bach, *St. Matthew Passion,* Blute nur, du liebes Herz

As mentioned above, several of the accents discussed individually often appear together. Below is an example of a typical combination of accents, in this case metric, dynamic, and pitch:

Example 147:   Beethoven, *Symphony No. 7 in A Major, Op. 92*, 1st Movement

A closer examination of the next example with respect to the accents which have been defined in this chapter results in an almost complete and rather convincing dynamic contour:

Example 148: Mozart, *Piano Sonata in A Minor, K. 310*, 2nd Movement

Definable accents in the above example:

1.   phrase accent

2.   embellishment
     dynamic   } accents
     metric

3.   texture accent

4.   harmonic   } accents
     metric

5.   embellishment   } accents
     dynamic

6.   harmonic   } accents
     metric

7.   embellishment   } accents
     harmonic

8.   embellishment figure, part of

9.   embellishment accent
     harmonic   } accents (effect of $^6_4$ chord)
     metric

Chapter Seven

MUSICAL PUNCTUATION; PHRASEOLOGY; FLOW AND MOMENTUM

PUNCTUATION IN SPEECH

When we speak, punctuation breaks the flow of words into meaningful segments: clauses, sentences, etc. Without audible punctuation, i.e., the rise and fall of the voice and the occasional silence—corresponding to commas, periods, and other punctuation marks—speech becomes a monotonous succession of syllables nearly incapable of delivering messages of significance.

Example 149: Sprague, Charles, "The American Indian," quoted in *Bartlett's Familiar Quotations*

Here lived and loved another race of beings. Beneath the same sun that rolls over your heads the Indian hunter pursued the panting deer . . . . The Indian of falcon glance and lion bearing, the theme of the touching ballad, the hero of the pathetic tale, is gone.

The taped examples illustrate how crucial proper punctuation is in all verbal communication. Version 149a on the tape is a continuous stream of words without punctuation. Version 149b does have punctuation-like inflections which, however, do not agree with the written punctuation. Only version 149c sounds convincing: punctuation has been meticulously observed, with the result that the meaning of the text is brought out clearly. Although the kinds of delivery illustrated in 149a and 149b make comprehension difficult if not impossible, they are not uncommon even among actors and lecturers.

MUSICAL PUNCTUATION; THE DEMARCATION OF MOTIVES AND PHRASES

In music, too, there is need of proper punctuation, though there are no exact equivalents for commas, periods, and the like. Notation, however, and the structure of music itself supply clues which enable the performer to achieve a clear demarcation of musical ideas. Without such demarcation—of motives, phrases,[1] etc.—music easily becomes a monotonous and nearly meaningless stream of notes.

What are some of the elements which serve as equivalents of punctuation, defining the boundaries of musical ideas?[2]

1.   Most obviously, rests separating motives or phrases:

Example 150: Beethoven, *Piano Sonata in C Major, Op. 2, No. 3*, 2nd Movement

2.   Repetitions of a motive or a phrase, whether exact (Ex. 151), or with alterations of pitch and/or rhythm, including sequences (Ex. 152). The beginning of the repetition also marks the end of the preceding motive or phrase as well as the boundary between them.

Example 151: J. S. Bach, *Cantata No. 68*, Mein gläubiges Herze

Example 152: Chopin, *Mazurka in A Minor, Op. 17, No. 4*

---

[1]A phrase is the musical equivalent of a clause or sentence in speech. The term "phrasing" should therefore properly be applied to the demarcation of phrases. Regrettably, it is most commonly used as a synonym for articulation, styles of bowing, and, in the case of singers and wind players, places to breathe. In order to avoid confusion it is best to use the term "articulation" when referring to the connection and separation of notes, and "phrase structure" and "phraseology" when discussing the demarcation of phrases.

[2]". . . phrasing is much like the subdivision of thought: its function is to link together subdivisions of musical thought (phrases) and to set them off from one another; it has thus the same function as punctuation marks in language" (Keller, *op. cit.,* p. 4).

Not all such repetitions involve noticeable gaps:

Example 153: Beethoven, *Piano Sonata in F Major, Op. 10, No. 2*, 3rd Movement

The fast tempo makes any separation of motives beyond the continuing *staccato* impractical. At a slower pace the last note of motive a would normally be shortened to separate it from its repetition (a₁).[3]

3.   Slurs indicating which notes belong together, their end denoting separation from the following groups:[4]

Example 154: Beethoven, *String Quartet in C Minor, Op. 18, No. 4*, 1st Movement

4.   Some changes of range and instrumentation.

5.   Cadences which clearly end a phrase, "conveying the impression of a momentary or permanent conclusion."[5]

---

[3]Ex. 166.

[4]Some of the slurs clearly imply punctuation, as at the end of the two initial phrases whose last notes should be shortened (●). Some serve mainly as bowing marks, without the gaps that punctuation usually entails: to ensure clear articulation of pitch repetitions, marked in the example with asterisks (*), and to allow for enough sound in an expressive passage such as this. The broken slurs (⌢ ⌢) indicate places where the melodic thrust requires continuity and the avoidance of any noticeable separation.

[5]Quoted from the *Harvard Dictionary of Music*.

Example 155: Mozart, *Piano Sonata in D Major, K. 284*, 3rd Movement

There is a half-cadence at bar 4 and a full cadence at bar 8.

6. Occasional interruptions of the rhythmic flow by means of *Luftpausen* or caesuras, fermatas, and general pauses (// , ' , G. P.), usually indicated by the composer.

The following is quoted here as a reminder that a change of punctuation may drastically affect meaning:

The teacher said the student is stupid.
"The teacher," said the student, "is stupid."[6]

Similarly, a shift in musical punctuation may play havoc with phraseology and musical logic.

IRREGULARITIES OF PHRASE CONSTRUCTION

As crucial as it is to recognize where punctuation is in order, it is equally important to be aware of structural irregularities in which punctuation is avoided or obscured.[7] Sometimes a connecting figure (marked by the bracket in the example below) will mask an otherwise obvious cadence.

---

[6]Stanton, Royal, *Steps in Singing for Voice Classes,* p. 89.
[7]Irregularities of phrase construction are rather extensively discussed in Keller, *op. cit.,* p. 21 ff.

Example 156:   Mozart, *Piano Sonata in D Major, K. 576*, 2nd Movement

Frequently individual phrases, which initially seem to conform to a "regular" four-bar pattern, upon closer inspection turn out to be shortened (elision, Ex. 157) or lengthened (extension, Ex. 158).

Example 157:   Beethoven, *Bagatelle, Op. 126, No. 2*

The second phrase (bars 35-41) begins like the first except for the slight melodic elaboration in bar 36 and the changed harmonic scheme; but its second half is contracted, so that instead of leading to a full cadence on bar 42, the eighth bar of the phrase, it ends on a half cadence on its seventh bar. The effect is not unlike a rhetorical question with its moment of silence abruptly broken by the violent figure of the opening passage.

Example 158: Beethoven, *Bagatelle, Op. 119, No. 1*

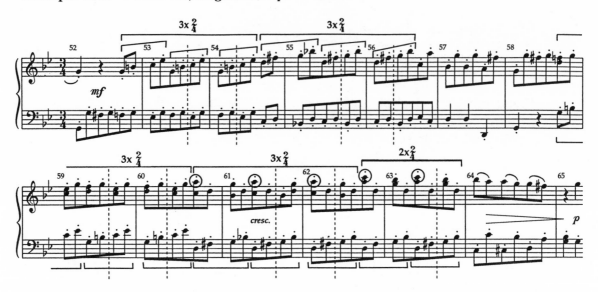

The main body of this Bagatelle consists of regular eight-bar groups, except for a four-bar retransition (bars 33-36). The episode beginning with bar 52, however, is anything but regular and fascinating enough to warrant more detailed discussion. It is a kind of mini-development section inserted before the codetta and based on motives first heard near the beginning:

Example 159:

The prevailing $\frac{3}{4}$ pattern is interrupted by repeated $\frac{2}{4}$ groupings, the iambic motives (♪♩ | ♪♩) marked by brackets and the underlying $\frac{2}{4}$ meter by extended broken bar lines. Beginning with bar 58, melody and bass of bars 52-57 are inverted. The extension in this case is actually an internal expansion,[8] marked with a thick-lined bracket.[9] The resolution following the considerable build-up of energy is withheld, occurring after a pause on the weak second beat. This "denouement" prepares the listener for the codetta, a less energetic, reflective restatement of the opening theme.

---

[8]For comparison see the extension in Ex. 171.

[9]One might take note of another rhythmic subtlety: determined by its position within the meter (bar 52), the motive is clearly iambic. During the second phrase, however, (bars 59-63) a shift seems to take place and one is inclined to hear trochees. This is due to three factors: (1) the continued weakening of the $\frac{3}{4}$ orientation; (2) the tension-relaxation relationship of dominant-tonic; and (3) the change in the melodic line, beginning with the pickup to bar 61, which gives prominence to the upper notes (encircled) in bars 61-63.

Adjoining phrases may be linked through a process sometimes called "dovetailing,"[10] in which the last bar of one phrase—which is elided—coincides with the first bar of the following phrase.

Example 160: Beethoven, *Egmont Overture*

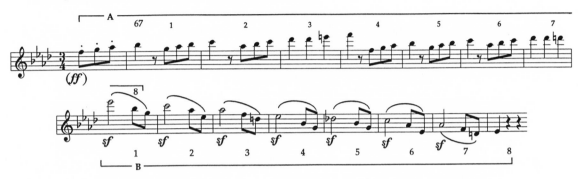

Because of the fast tempo the ¾ measures are felt as *Grosstakte* of four bars each, Phrase A with the scheme l-h-l-h—l-h-l-h, Phrase B, h-l-l-h (or, possibly, h-l-h-l)—h-l-l-h. Bar 8 of Phrase A (bar 74) is elided and replaced with bar 1 of Phrase B (a typical example of "dovetailing").

Phrases occasionally overlap, as invariably happens in fugues and other imitative counterpoint, when one voice enters before another has completed its phrase.

Example 161: J. S. Bach, *The Well-Tempered Clavier, Vol. II,* Fuga a 4 in E Major

Such structural irregularities which reflect a composer's ingenuity and skill provide surprises and unending fascination for the listener, but only if the performer is aware of them and manages to expose and project them through appropriate inflections of dynamics, tempo, articulation, etc.

FLOW IN MUSIC; FOCAL POINTS

An awareness of the elements of musical punctuation not only allows the performer to map out the musical ideas of a composition and to define its structure, it also helps him establish

---

[10]The term is borrowed from carpentry.

the sense of flow without which a piece of music cannot truly come alive. Musicians frequently use the words "flow" and "momentum" when discussing musical performance; yet their exact meaning is not easily defined. One may compare flow in music to the flow of water in a stream: gathering momentum or barely drifting along, depending on the incline or occasional obstacles, but moving on inexorably toward its destination.

As in so many other instances, speech provides an illuminating analogy. In the following example clauses and sentences are clearly set off by punctuation marks; but it is the high point—the points of strongest emphasis (marked $\downarrow$)—toward which speech flows, and it is this flow which supplies vitality and much of the meaning.

Example 162: Stevens, Wallace, "Sunday Morning," IV, in *Six American Poets*, ed. Joel Connaroe

She says, "I am content when wakened birds,
Before they fly, test the reality
Of misty fields, by their sweet questionings;
But when the birds are gone, and their warm fields
Return no more, where, then, is paradise?"[11]

We have encountered this phenomenon earlier in the book in our examination of accentual patterns.[12]

Flow is not synonymous with pace; it is rather the sense of movement from one point to another and, more specifically, from one prominent accent to the next. We shall call such accents "focal points."[13] In essence, the phenomenon under consideration here is one of dynamics.

Each phrase has its focal point. Once phrases and their focal points have been identified, the various focal points of the larger segments of a composition may be evaluated and compared in order to determine their relative prominence and thereby the ebb and flow of the entire piece. While flow in music does not manifest itself in obvious and concrete ways, the listener is usually aware of its presence. In that case the performance has vitality, it is arresting and evocative. When it is absent the performance seems bland and mechanical.

The example below is recorded in two versions, illustrating performances with (Ex. 163a on the tape) and without some of the nuances responsible for a sense of flow. There is movement in Example 163b, in keeping with the prevailing rhythmic pulsation; but the performance seems static, lacking flow and momentum.

---

[11]Different individuals may find points of emphasis in other, or additional, places; but the principle in force here remains unchanged.
[12]See the Shakespeare Sonnet in Chapter Three, p. 34.
[13]In the examples the focal points are indicated with vertical arrows ($\downarrow$).

Example 163: Beethoven, *Bagatelle, Op. 126, No. 1*

STRUCTURAL ANALYSIS AND PERFORMANCE

The process of identifying the phraseology of a piece and the elements which determine flow and momentum involves analytical procedures. The kind of analysis, however, which is essential in molding a performance differs from the analytical procedures music students are generally taught in the course of their studies.

There is no question that every performer needs to know how a piece of music is put together, since **most interpretive decisions are based on structural elements**. Without an understanding of these elements interpretation largely remains a matter of guesswork and accident. But even a thorough grasp of the structural facets of a composition will not lead to valid and convincing music-making, unless the performer is able to relate these structural facets to elements of performance.   The two kinds of analysis, applied to the following excerpt, illustrate the differences in orientation and purpose. As will be seen, in terms of interpretation the first approach (Ex. 164) is nearly irrelevant, for the various structural components are examined piecemeal (and even out of order when, e.g., all the occurrences of a particular motive are sought out and tabulated). The analysis then remains a mere auditing procedure in which the implications for performance are virtually ignored. The factor of tempo barely enters the picture, and if dynamics are considered at all, they, too, remain secondary and usually are neglected.

When it comes to performance, however, **almost all interpretive decisions depend on the performer's sense of the unfolding of the music in time, on an awareness of the musical events as they occur in their proper order**. And it is the nature and arrangement of the accentual patterns which determine flow and momentum—from the smallest iambic or trochaic patterns and the like to those of phrases and larger segments.

Example 164: Mozart, *Symphony No. 40 in G Minor, K. 550*, 1st Movement

To be sure, an analysis which identifies the motives, the phraseology (determined here by the rests), and the harmonic progressions of a piece brings out important facts concerning its structure. These facts in themselves, however, tell us little about the interpretation. It is only as we shift our orientation that the implications for performance reveal themselves.

Example 164a: 1st violins only

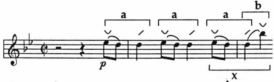

1. Motive a is iambic (◡ │), motive b trochaic (│ ◡). One may also think of the figure marked x as an amphibrach (middle-accented, ◡│◡), rather than a dovetailing of motives a and b. Hearing the motives in terms of movement, i.e., with direction toward and away from their respective accents, is the first step toward establishing a sense of flow.

2. The rhythmic configuration of the initial phrases conforms to the basic meter with its familiar accent scheme (see Chapter Three, p. 31).

Example 164b:

3.   It does not take much experimentation to realize that, particularly because of the fast tempo and the *alla breve* (¢), the theme is heard in groups of two bars (*Grosstakt*),[14] with the main accents falling on the downbeats of bars 3, 5, etc. Concerning the relative weight of the individual bars the designations "heavy" and "light" are also useful (abbreviated h and l).[15]

Example 164c:

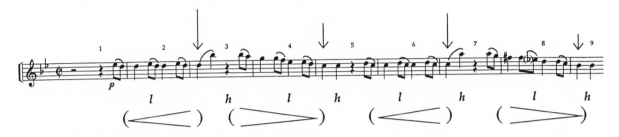

4.   The focal points thus occur on the downbeats of bars 3, 5, 7, and 9. If one focuses one's attention on the melody, one is likely to put the main emphasis on bar 3, following a build-up of energy through the repeat of motive a. This buildup culminates in the high pitch of the phrase which, however, is softer than the downbeat since it occurs on the second, the unaccented quarter, not unlike an energetic rebound. The second phrase with its descending pattern represents a relaxation. The subsequent phrases form a sequence to the first pair, one step lower and therefore on a lesser level of energy. The size of the vertical arrows indicates the relative prominence of the focal points. There are subtle implied crescendos on bars 2 and 6 and corresponding decrescendos on bars 4 and 8.

Another way of hearing this passage is found by focusing on the underlying harmonic progressions. The first change of harmony occurs on bar 5 (II $^6_2$), the second on bar 7 (V $^6_5$), followed by the V$_7$, with the tonic returning on bar 9. In the progression I II $^6_2$ V $^6_5$ V$_7$ I the II $^6_2$ represents the greatest relative tension and thus, in terms of harmonic activity, the main focal point. The pattern of focal points then turns out to be:

Example 164d:

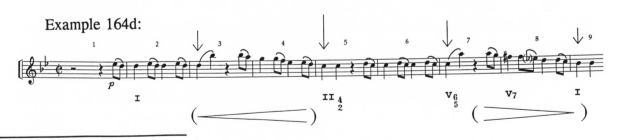

---

[14]See Chapter Three, p. 32.
[15]See also p. 33.

111

Either version is convincing as long as the dynamics are adjusted, in keeping with the preferred scheme. These dynamic nuances are, of course, quite subtle; but properly applied—without romantic exaggeration—they make the performance infinitely more interesting and expressive than if the *p* marked in the score is strictly and mechanically observed throughout the passage.

One more element should be included in this "performance analysis," the articulation. The markings—here mainly bowing marks—are explicit enough; but the violinists should take care not to separate the slurred eighth notes from the following quarters, and shorten the quarters only slightly so that the lyrical flow of the music is not impaired. The second of the quarter notes, on bars 3, 5, 7, and 9 should also be lightened and shortened, as is appropriate in feminine groups.

It is useful to examine further the respective purposes and orientation of the two approaches to analysis. Here again language provides a parallel, in this case through the difference in emphasis between writing and recitation. The writer concentrates on the manner in which words are put together. He has to pay attention to grammar and syntax in order to get his basic message across; but in general he will consider the actual delivery—the recitation—only peripherally. The actor or speaker, however, is mainly concerned with the particulars of delivery—pace, accentuation, inflection of volume and the like, i.e., all the elements which project and dramatize the meaning of the text.

The difference in emphasis between composer and performer is very similar to that between writer and actor or speaker. In creating a piece of music the composer focuses his attention primarily on such elements as melodic shapes, harmonic progressions, rhythmic schemes, structural design and instrumentation, but less so on the elements of performance—those subject to interpretation (in other words, the variables of music such as tempo, dynamics, and articulation). The performer, however, concentrates on these very elements, and generally concerns himself with the structural elements of the music only as they have bearing on his performance.

In analyzing a passage one may be prone to separate successive motives and phrases which in performance should be linked. In order to assure flow and continuity the performer has to be aware of the momentum set up by a motive or phrase and follow it through to its logical point of destination; for **every motive and phrase creates its own momentum and its own sense of expectation**. This phenomenon can perhaps best be understood through an analogy from sports: predictably and inevitably, when a ball is thrown it rises and drops according to its initial direction, speed, rotation, the wind direction and force, and, of course, gravity. The phenomena and the modifying factors are very different, but the parallel is useful. Whenever a performer is aware of the momentum generated by a motive or phrase, he will make the continuation more convincing and maintain the necessary flow inherent in any piece of music.

In summary, analysis is an essential tool of the performer, for almost all of the details of a score affect interpretation. But he must make sure that the quasi-statistical findings of structural analysis never remain ends in themselves, unrelated to performance, and are always translated into elements of interpretation. The examples below will demonstrate ways of dealing with typical problems of punctuation and flow, such as:

1. Identifying motives and the manner in which they combine into phrases;

2. Taking note of the punctuation between them, from notated rests to the subtlest separation;

3. Assessing the structure of phrases and recognizing irregular groupings (linkages of various kinds, elisions, extension, etc.);

4. Finding the focal points and determining their relative prominence;

5. Plotting the subtle adjustments in dynamics and articulation which produce musical flow and "bring music to life."

The number of our examples is limited, but the ramifications of their discussion should combine into a frame of reference ample enough to enable the performer to approach any interpretive challenge with confidence. The nuances involved are invariably subtle, but the difference between a "neutral" and mechanical rendition and a "musical" performance in each case is unmistakable and striking.

Example 165: J. S. Bach, *Partita No. 2 in C Minor*, Allemande.

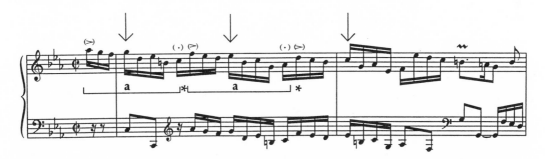

Motive a consists of an anacrusis of three sixteenths followed by a group of five sixteenths, the first of which is its focal point (↓). The melody drops by a 6th, except for the up-turn at the barline and the slight undulation, and has its energy renewed, so to speak, by the upward skip of a 4th (*), at which point the motive is repeated sequentially. Motive a extends from anacrusis to anacrusis, cutting across the barline. Emphasizing the first note (⇒) and shortening the last (·) clarifies its boundary and adds impetus (Ex. 165a on the tape). Simply "playing the notes" and grouping them in fours according to the beams (⊓⊓), while ignoring the rhythmic and melodic configuration of the motive, sounds mechanical and unnatural (165b).

Example 166: J. S. Bach, *Overture in the French Manner,* Bourrée I

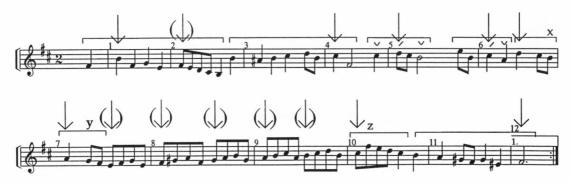

The two-bar phrases at the beginning, marked by brackets, conform to the anacrusis pattern typical of the bourrée. The two following shorter groups (amphibrachs) seem designed to bring about a change from the anacrusis pattern to strong-beat oriented figures (marked x and y), with accents on the first and third beats of each bar. A series of sequential repetitions then leads to what sounds like the end of a bourrée phrase (z), but a complete bourrée phrase (marked by another bracket) does not occur until the end of the section. The first two focal points are easily identified (although the first of them could be construed to fall on the downbeat of either bar 1 or bar 2). Other than the minor accents, marked by smaller arrows, all prominent points of emphasis are suppressed until the final point of destination at bar 12.

Example 167: Brahms, *Clarinet Trio in A Minor, Op. 114*, 1st Movement

The slurs in this example suggest a separation of the two-note motives in bars 1 and 2; but after some experimentation (preferably singing the entire phrase up to bar 5 in one breath) it will become clear that the slurs are intended as bowing marks assuring enough tone for this beautiful, sweeping phrase. The cellist should think of one long expressive *legato* (indicated by the broken slur) and use slight leaning accents at the points marked (⌢) to produce the characteristic combination of vigor and lyricism. Because of the fast pace and the *alla breve* the first four measures combine into a *Grosstakt*, with the following distribution of weight (h, 1) and focal points (the main emphasis falls on either bar 2 or 4, depending on the performer's preference):

Example 167a:

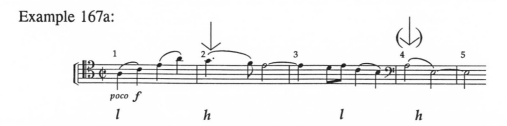

Example 168: Beethoven, *Piano Sonata in E flat Major, Op. 7*, 2nd Movement

In this mini-example the initial two-note motive would normally be played as a trochee (∤ ͧ), with the eighth note on "2" softer than the downbeat. But it is obviously meant to form a phrase together with its dotted variant in bar 2. In order to generate the momentum to bridge the long rest (ʔ ≀), the eighth note has to be somewhat louder. This also sounds more satisfactory, since the melody rises and the dominant seventh chord (*), following the tonic triad, represents an increase in harmonic tension. Bar 2 mirrors bar 1, in terms of both dynamics and flow, through the rise and fall of the melody and the increase and decrease of harmonic tension.

Example 169: Schumann, *Piano Quintet*, 2nd Movement

It is likely that the composer put the *p* at the beginning, and in the violin part *molto piano* in order to hint at the somber mood of the passage and to impose some restraint on the performer. Playing the entire passage on one dynamic level, however, is uninteresting and even somewhat unnatural. A few subtle dynamic inflections—within a very narrow range, of course—make a great deal of difference. A slight *crescendo* on the repeat of motive a and the resulting increase in tension prepare the listener for the upward leaps and the added excitement of the sixteenths which lead to the climax of the phrase, its focal point. A repetition such as that of motive a (bar 3) is often quite properly played softer, as a kind of echo. In this context, however, this would make the continuation sound unprepared and unmotivated.

The question arises whether the repeat of the four-bar phrase—in the 1st violin part entirely identical—should also sound exactly the same. The answer is found in the underlying harmonic progressions. At bar 6 there is a deceptive cadence. The unexpected A♭ triad (VI) wants to be somewhat emphasized and the following chords, especially the VII $^{\circ}_{7}$, inject an element of tension which puts decidedly more weight on the second phrase. $^{6}_{5}$

The following example proves even more conclusively that the context determines how a motive is shaped in performance (in terms of dynamics and articulation) and how otherwise identical statements of a motive can—and should—sound quite different.

Example 170: Haydn, *Symphony No. 95 in C Minor*, 1st Movement

116

The focal point of the phrase bars 4 to 7 is on the downbeat of bar 6 (↓), which is also the accented part of a feminine ending. The run-on figure (motive a) represents merely an elaboration of its weak, unaccented portion. The following motive a_1, also bracketed, is—apart from the transposition—identical with a; but in performance it sounds quite different because of its function as anacrusis to the next focal point and its changed position in the larger rhythmic scheme. The implied dynamics are exactly opposite: motive a calls for a *decrescendo*, a_1 for a *crescendo*. Played with these inflections, the theme sounds lively and charming, without them somewhat bland.

The entire passage, from the beginning of the movement, is striking in the contrasts as well as the irregularity of the phrases. The opening motto with its long rhetorical pause at first seems to have nothing to do with the main theme; but it does return, earlier than expected (elision), to form a dramatic frame for the theme.

Example 171: Brahms: *Violin Sonata in A Major, No. 2, Op. 100*, 1st Movement

The slurs of all four measures of this theme, virtually exuding Brahmsian warmth, all stop at the barline.[16] It should immediately become obvious, however, that there must be no separation—and no routine bar accent—so that the music flows uninterruptedly to the end of the fourth measure, and actually of the fifth (formally an extension). Here again flow will be enhanced if the four measures are made to sound like one *Grosstakt* (h 1 1 h or 1 h 1 h).

Example 172: Beethoven, *Symphony No. 1 in C Major, Op. 21*, 2nd Movement

---

[16]See also Ex. 85, p. 72.

The tape offers a generally satisfactory version of this famous excerpt (Ex. 172a). Once in a while, however, one hears it played in such a way that the repeated notes are grouped as marked by the broken line (Ex. 172b). This is obviously wrong in view of the anacrusis nature of motive a which begins with an eighth note pick-up and ends before its repeat (forming an amphibrach). The two-note slur suggests a phrase accent on the pickup note ($>$) and a shortening and relative lightening of the downbeat. But if the accents are too pronounced and the *staccato* notes too short, the phrase (bars 1-4) sounds broken up and fussy. With the extreme opposite approach it sounds weak and sentimental (Exs. 172c and 172d on the tape). Experimentation will help in determining the appropriate degree of accentuation, articulation, and flow. It should also be noted that viola and cello enter before the theme is completed (*). This is an example of phrase overlapping, typically encountered in fugues and imitative counterpoint.

Example 173: Mozart, *Marriage of Figaro,* Overture, piano reduction

118

One often hears the beginning of this Overture played *pp*, without dynamic inflections whatsoever. The effect is striking enough, but does not begin to match the magic of a performance which brings out the subtle choreography of Mozart's lines. First of all, it is only natural to let motive a taper off ($\Longrightarrow$), rather than sustain the *pp* without inflection. The figure in bar 2 then rises with a minuscule *crescendo* toward the repeat of motive a in bar 3, a fifth higher. Bar 4 functions like bar 2, except that the line does not rise but drops to bar 5 which repeats the figure in bar 4 sequentially. Bar 6 then continues the eighth notes with an upturn at the end. This passage seems most convincing when there are minute metric accents on the downbeats of bars 1 and 3 and practically none on those of bars 4, 5, and 6, the melodic drop being accompanied by a slight *decrescendo*. Because of the *Presto alla breve* the first phrase is heard in 2-bar groups. Bar 8, however, which one would expect to complete a "regular" 8-bar phrase, has been elided and replaced with the first of a 4-bar group leading to the climax of the section, on bar 12. Actually the fast tempo and the 2-bar grouping established in the beginning make one hear the dotted half-notes in the oboes as off-beat accents of the larger measures (marked by extended bar-lines). The *fortissimo* downbeat of bar 12 is the climax of the first segment which sounds early and unexpected because of another elision. It also marks the beginning of a 6-bar phrase which utilizes the rhythm of bar 8 (with eighth notes on the fourth quarter) and, after an energetic repeated foreshortening of its melody, leads to the return of the opening motive.

The opening of the Overture is a miracle of inventiveness and charm. With all details properly revealed it sounds so convincing, so inevitable that it is a shock to realize its structure is quite irregular.

SEEING THE FOREST *AND* THE TREES

It is easy to become so wrapped up in details that one loses sight of the larger picture, that one "cannot see the forest for the trees." To find a balance between attention to detail and continuity and flow, and to project every musical idea clearly while exposing the larger design and the full scope of an extended composition is a constant challenge for any performer.

The term "overphrasing" is aptly applied to a performance in which motives and even individual notes are given more importance than their position and function within the larger structure warrants. Usually this is done through exaggerated dynamic swells and overly pronounced articulation. Sometimes the effect is further aggravated by *rubato*-like tempo fluctuations. "Overphrasing" is only the exaggerated opposite of a performance which lacks nuance and is insensitive and mechanical.

Interpretations vary enormously; but in this context, too, it will be helpful to think of an area of appropriateness in order to avoid excesses: being overly concerned with details, on one hand, overdoing punctuation, and slighting them on the other to such a degree that the performance becomes glib and shallow.

ABSENCE OF PUNCTUATION: *OSTINATO*

Ostinatos of recurring melody patterns can be found relatively frequently. Only rarely, however, do composers set up series of identical repeated notes—or chords—without any metric organization or punctuation whatever, merely as a continuous pulsation. In such *ostinato* passages barlines and time signatures seem to serve no purpose other than to facilitate counting.[17] Putting accents on downbeats belies the intent of the composer and destroys the effect of the pulsation in providing the background against which the specific rhythm patterns are set—much as the subject of a painting against a uniform background.

The two famous excerpts below are examples of such an undifferentiated pulsation and make their point only if all accents are avoided: in Example 174 until the change of harmony (marked *), and in Example 175 well beyond the entrance of the theme, which has its own

Example 174: Beethoven, *Piano Sonata in C Major, Op. 53, Waldstein,* 1st Movement

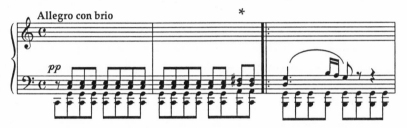

Example 175: Beethoven, *Symphony No. 8 in F Major, Op. 93,* 2nd Movement

---

[17]See also p. 89.

phraseology without affecting the *ostinato*-pulsation in the accompanying instruments.

The following excerpt has been included here and analyzed in some detail, because it is a rare and arresting example of such an *ostinato* dominating most of the piece. Motives and phrase structure are designed to make the rhythm of the "substantive" material run counter to the time signature for the better part of the page.

Example 176: Bartók, *Mikrokosmos, Volume VI,* Ostinato

The low "D" in bar 5 introduces the first true rhythmic event. It is one of several such "Ds" which, hammered out properly, set up patterns (meters) of five eighths. At first glance the initial time signature and the regularly spaced bar lines make the $\frac{2}{4}$ meter appear constant; but what the listener actually hears is fascinatingly capricious music consisting of the following:

1.   A series of undifferentiated eighth-note pulses;

2.   A group of single-note accents ("D") spaced five eighths apart;

3.   A phrase made up of motivic fragments (bars 8-12 incl.), repeated with modifications (this is further discussed below);

4.   The group of accents on "D" repeated;

5.   A restatement of the double-phrase (bars 8-16) at the higher octave, but with significant changes which, for the first time, allow a continuous $\frac{2}{4}$ meter to assert itself.

The brackets in Example 176 suggest the various rhythmic groupings (meters) the listener hears, if the *sforzato* is in each case understood to represent the true downbeat (marked also with broken barlines). If the downbeats of bars 10, 12, and 14 are accented in order to emphasize the nature of the segment, the *sforzatos* in bars 10 and 14 are heard as syncopations. This latter version, however, sounds fussier and less convincing. One of the reasons is that the sixteenth notes in bars 10 and 12, being shorter, should also be lighter than the surrounding eighths, particularly when approached in stepwise motion.

Chapter Eight

THE STUDY AND TEACHING OF MUSICAL INTERPRETATION

The preceding chapters (Chapters Two through Seven) are organized in such a way that the student can focus his attention on one element of interpretation at a time, in the process getting a thorough understanding and an overview of all its facets. Together these chapters make up a compendium of the interpretive elements of performance.

This chapter deals with the pedagogical aspects of interpretation.

ESSENTIAL PREMISES AND GROUND RULES

1. The score can tell much more about its interpretation than meets the eye.

2. **It is the only tangible product of a composer's creative labors and the only true source concerning his ideas about its performance.** Only the score can reveal how the notes and symbols the composer put down should be transformed into sound. Unless a performer respects the composer's authority, he is likely to stop short of grasping the subtler and more profound implications of the score.

    Toscanini used to say that every time he looked at a Beethoven score he discovered something new (after having conducted it hundreds of times!). Almost every musician goes through similar experiences time and again, which confirms that continued study and reexamination of a score invariably adds to one's insight and depth of understanding.

3. The performer must—from the earliest stages in the study of interpretation in general and in tackling a new piece—learn to recognize the clues the score itself provides concerning its interpretation.

4. Once he has established the necessary interpretive concepts, he must strive to hear mentally the music he is about to perform, creating in effect an "aural blueprint" to which to match his performance.

5. From the earliest stage possible the performer must also learn to monitor the sounds he actually produces. Only then can he mold his performance to please himself and his listeners while doing justice to the music.

6. **Technique is only a means to an end—which is to "make music."** Accuracy, velocity, even beautiful sounds alone create only a shallow "perfection." It is the interpretation which breathes soul into a performance and gives it meaning. It is what affects the listener, providing inspiration and uplift, diversion and entertainment, according to the spirit and character of the music.

7. Talent and natural aptitude obviously play a role in the development of interpretive skills, but do not eliminate nor even lessen the need for care and diligence.

FUNDAMENTAL CONCEPTS REVIEWED

1. Except for pitches and basic time values all other elements in the score are "variables": tempo markings, dynamics and accents, articulation marks, etc.[1]

2. The specific values or levels of variables must be kept within the "area of appropriateness,"[2] in other words, adjusted to the context of a passage.

3. The principles of basic musical rhetoric, as discussed in Chapter Three, must always be applied.

Just knowing that the context of a passage will determine the dynamic level of a note or an accent, or the rate of *crescendo* or *diminuendo*, or the length of a *staccato* note, etc., will make the performer more sensitive to the subtler implications of a score and its markings.

"INSTANT INTERPRETATION"

When learning to deal with the variables effectively the performer becomes accustomed to making choices and exercising his judgment. Gradually this process becomes a well-practiced and virtually automatic routine. Ultimately, what started out as a laborious, time-consuming effort, becomes an almost spontaneous, nearly intuitive response to the score—instant interpretation, as it were. This is, of course, how experienced musicians manage to give convincing and polished performances at first sight.

WHEN TO INTRODUCE ELEMENTS OF INTERPRETATION

An experienced teacher knows better than to dwell on interpretive subtleties before his student can play or sing a piece with reasonable accuracy; but to try and achieve technical "perfection" first and only then "add the interpretation" is equally ill-advised. **The more deeply patterns of execution are ingrained, the more difficult it is to change them, and every change of volume, tempo, articulation, punctuation, etc., also requires technical adjustments.** In order to avoid major corrections and save much time and effort, it is therefore essential to bring technical and interpretive elements together at an early stage.

The first steps in acquainting oneself with a piece of music may be compared to an actor's initial reading of a text. The words will be understood and its basic message will come across; but until some thought is given to character analysis and development, and to the

---

[1]See Chapter One, pp. 1 and 2.
[2]See Chapter One, p. 4.

implications of the setting, dramatic content and interplay, there can be no meaningful interpretation.

Similarly, the first steps in preparing a piece of music for performance will have the purpose of getting the notes into place. If the interpretation in this initial stage is somewhat tentative, it is perhaps just as well. As long as the performer can be secure in the knowledge that his first "blueprint" is fundamentally correct—i.e., pitches in order, basic time values accurate, some marks of expression and articulation being observed—it may be an advantage to leave options open concerning dynamic and tempo fluctuations, subtleties of phrasing and articulation, etc., until there has been a chance to digest thoroughly all the evidence the score has to offer.

STAGES IN THE PREPARATION FOR "MUSICAL" PERFORMANCE

When taking up a new piece a student will focus his attention on the following—as will any experienced musician looking at a score for the first time:

I. 1. Time signature, meter and/or beat pattern ($\frac{6}{8}$ may be in 2 or 6, $\frac{9}{8}$ in 9 or 3, etc.);[3]

2. Key signature, pitches, and time values;

3. Tempo markings;

4. Printed marks of expression (dynamics, accents, and verbal indications);

5. Printed articulation marks.

Merely seeing and absorbing all that is printed in the score provides the best possible start toward effective performance.

II. A second stage involves applying principles of

1. Basic musical rhetoric (outlined in Chapter Three), and

2. Punctuation and musical flow (Chapter Seven).

---

[3]The time signature does not necessarily reflect the true meter underlying a passage. In an *allegro molto* $\frac{3}{4}$, for example, each measure will receive one beat only, in a *Grosstakt*-pattern which is reflected in the sounds of the actual performance (and, in the case of orchestral and choral music, in the conductor's beat pattern as well).

Further refinement in a performer's interpretation will come about in the degree that he deals with the elements listed below:[4]

III. 1. The specific metronomic implications of tempo markings; the actual rate of acceleration and deceleration (*accelerando, ritardando*, etc.) and other tempo fluctuations; the execution of *rubato*; the actual length of fermatas;

2. Shifting meters and groupings differing from the printed meter and independent of the barring scheme;

3. The subtler dynamic implications of rhythmic groupings, of barring, of durational values, of syncopation, of the *Grosstakt* where applicable; "heavy" and "light" measures;

4. Assigning specific dynamic values, preferably in numerals, whether dynamic markings are present or not; the rate of *crescendo* and *decrescendo*; vertical balances; the dynamic implications of harmonic activity;

5. The degree of separation of notes not slurred (their actual duration); the degree and character of an attack, apart from its dynamic level; the shaping of long notes in the case of sustaining instruments and the voice; *legato* for non-sustaining instruments;

6. The intensity and color of sounds irrespective of dynamic levels;

7. Structural analysis: identifying motives and phrases and their boundaries; finding focal points and establishing a basis for musical flow;

8. "Putting it all together:" the interaction of elements such as pace and articulation, dynamics and articulation, harmonic activity and dynamics, vertical blending vs. clarity of individual lines; the balance between attention to detail and the larger structural aspects (avoidance of overphrasing on one hand, and glib virtuosity on the other).

THE ACT OF PERFORMANCE

The act of performance—actually, every instant in the performance of a piece of music—consists of four phases:

---

[4]All the elements ennumerated here are fully discussed in the pertinent chapters.

1.   Plotting its progress;

2.   The physical actions which produce the sounds the listener hears;

3.   Monitoring—by the performer—of the sounds produced by the instruments and/or voices, in effect a kind of feedback;

4.   Molding the performance by making adjustments and corrections on the basis of this feedback.

The details of this process can perhaps best be understood in terms of the conductor's function:

1.   He conducts, according to interpretive concepts previously established through careful study and analysis;

2.   Orchestra and/or chorus play and sing according to his gestures;

3.   The conductor monitors—by listening intently—the sounds actually produced;

4.   He modifies succeeding conducting gestures, if necessary, to have the players' and singers' responses conform to his concepts.

Any soloist functions similarly, except that the interaction between conductor and performers—separate individuals—here is concentrated in one individual fulfilling the functions of both conductor and performer. The actions described are so closely bound up with one another that a clear-cut division into several phases almost seems a futile intellectual exercise. That, however, is emphatically not the case, particularly when compared to a very familiar sequence of events, each of which is not only recognized as a separate action but also practiced separately: a batter takes his stance, grips his bat and swings it, according to innumerable strategy and practice sessions. If he connects, he checks the direction of the ball, drops the bat and runs. All these actions and reactions take only fractions of a second.

This is only one of many analogous processes which involve plotting a course of action, the actions themselves, and the necessary monitoring and feedback to allow for corrections.

STEPS TOWARD EFFECTIVE SELF-STUDY AND INDEPENDENCE

It has been hinted before that only by asking questions can a teacher be sure to engage the mind of the student. Another benefit of this (Socratic) approach, methodically applied, is that the student generally becomes aware of the range of problems any score poses as well as the clues it provides toward their solution. In time he becomes accustomed to this process to such a degree that he continues on his own to scrutinize a new score, analyzing it as if the teacher were still present, asking questions. This is, of course, what any mature musician does. The Socratic method, consistently applied, thus leads to independence. In other words, **the performer trained in this manner will not wait helplessly until he has heard a new piece played in order to imitate someone else's interpretation.**

THE FEAR OF "OVER-REHEARSING"

Some musicians are afraid of "over-rehearsing" and "going stale." When first learning a piece, one necessarily has to establish kinesthetic patterns—i.e., basic technical responses—through repetition; but once some control has been achieved, there should be no further repetition without specific purpose, whether correcting mistakes or adjusting details. Other than mindless repetition which does produce inattention and boredom, lack of spontaneity in a performance is usually due to other factors: lack of preparation altogether, lack of concentration and, above all, lack of a clear concept of the music and therefore a lack of conviction about its interpretation. How is it otherwise possible that busy conductors and concert artists, who spend countless hours studying and practicing in addition to exacting concert schedules, manage to sound spontaneous and inspired throughout crowded seasons of appearances year after year? **It is thorough preparation, a complete grasp of the score, and utter conviction concerning its interpretation which provide security and allow for true abandon in performance.**

"COMMANDING INSPIRATION"

Unlike a masterpiece of visual art—a painting or a sculpture—which inspires by its very presence, a piece of music achieves reality only through performance. At the moment of re-creation it exists only as a series of images in the mind of the performer. It is the quality of these images which determines the level of the performance.

When a performer understands and loves a piece of music and is himself inspired by it, his performance is likely to be inspired. Being filled with the spirit of the music and in a state of heightened awareness and exultation, as well as total concentration, he will not be distracted. And it is this combination of an all-encompassing understanding of the music and a passionate identification with its spirit and all its manifestations that produces inspired performances. Just focusing on the spirit of the music means, in effect, "commanding inspiration."

ATTENTION TO DETAIL AND SUCCESSFUL PERFORMANCE

The performance of some Olympic champions demonstrates stunning control as well as total abandon. When equally outstanding athletes falter, the difference between success and failure seems only one of confidence.

The books *The Inner Game of Tennis* and *The Inner Game of Music*, respectively by W. Timothy Gallway and Barry Green (see "Selected Bibliography," p. 137), on the whole very helpful to performers in many fields, quite properly warn against preoccupation with details during performance, which more often than not interferes with its success. Unfortunately, many young and inexperienced performers believe that preoccupation with detail in itself may produce failure. But without a thorough study of the details of a score and a clear concept of its interpretive aspects a performer is unlikely to succeed in any case. If he knows, however, that he has mastered all technical and interpretive problems, he will be secure and confident in performance.

DOING THE WRONG THING DELIBERATELY

The road to perfection is rarely straight. In striving toward the peak of one's performance one often learns as much or more from mistakes and failures than by going from one success to another. When in doubt about the solution to a problem it is actually useful to do the wrong thing deliberately, if only to determine what to avoid. One can also try to overshoot the mark, so to speak, and then aim short (too fast and too slow, too loud and too soft, too long and too short, etc.). This process of "zeroing in" is, of course, only another way of identifying the "area of appropriateness."

NURTURING CONFIDENCE AND ENTHUSIASM

It is particularly important that younger students and less experienced performers don't allow themselves to be overwhelmed by the complexities of musical performance. They should remind themselves that training in all areas of the performing arts, and sports as well, requires perseverance, concentration, and patience in honing the many diverse skills which together produce satisfying performances.

On the whole, there must be a gentle and gradual progression from the general to the specific, and from limited interpretive requirements to more complete and detailed directions for performance. Above all, **love and enthusiasm for music must not be stifled.** The necessary emphasis on thoroughness and meticulousness in study and practice must not turn into the kind of pedantry which impedes progress and reduces the pleasures of making music to drudgery.

"PRACTICING" INTERPRETATION

A conductor by necessity does his preliminary study and practice without orchestra or chorus. In one respect this is an advantage: he can focus his attention on the interpretation alone, without being in any way distracted by problems of technique, control and interaction. Having done his groundwork and acquired a thorough grasp of the score and its interpretive requirements, he can read and/or think through the work, or conduct it as if he were confronting a group. Each time he goes through such a practice-performance, he will strengthen his grasp of the interpretation and in turn become more secure about his own concept of the music.

The instrumentalist or singer as a rule will deal with the interpretation as he plays or sings through a piece. Here, too, however, it will be an advantage to read or hum, or simply think through the piece without actually playing or singing, so that any preoccupation with technical matters is avoided. This process invariably clarifies the performer's concepts, strengthens his grasp, and enhances his performance.

ATTRIBUTES OF A TEACHER OF INTERPRETATION

The following are attributes of a good teacher in any field, but especially the teacher of musical interpretation (including the conductor whose role it is to get the individuals under his direction to share his vision and function in a manner and on a level they would not attain without his catalytic skills):

1. A commitment to the student irrespective of level and talent;

2. The conviction that every student of normal intelligence and coordination has the potential to improve and raise the level of his performance;

3. The ability to make the student believe in himself while rousing in him the expectation of accomplishment and success;

4. The ability to identify problems and to assist the student in finding solutions for every one of them;

5. The capacity to inspire the student and stimulate his imagination so that "making music" becomes the only meaningful goal, *not* merely playing the notes, no matter how proficiently;

6. A respect for the student's individuality and the willingness to allow him to develop his own artistic personality;

7. To be flexible, avoiding any Procrustean[5] approach, while insisting on "musical" performance.

---

[5]Procrustes, an evil giant in Greek mythology, forced his victims to lie on a bed too short for them and then cut off whatever overlapped. If the bed proved too long, he would stretch them to fit its length.

Chapter Nine

IMAGINATION AND THE USE OF IMAGERY

What is the difference between a stirring performance which has an audience spellbound and one which seems perfectly correct but leaves everybody cool and uninvolved? In describing such performances most people will speak of inspiration, artistry, and talent, on the one hand, and deplore the lack of them, on the other. Often it is simply put this way: "some performers have it, and others don't." But "it"—meaning talent—comes in many shades, all the way from little and limited to superior and miraculous.

TALENT AND IMAGINATION

Talent is obviously a factor in musical performance, as it is in drama, ballet, or athletics. Its presence, however, in whatever degree, can only be acknowledged; it can neither be taught nor learned.

The question then arises if there are other factors involved in the process of transforming bland performances into vital and compelling ones, and making artists out of indifferent performers. One such factor, above all, is imagination.

Imagination, like talent, is commonly regarded as a somewhat nebulous phenomenon. Nevertheless, one of its functions can be understood in simple, practical terms. Imagination has to do with images as the word implies, and images are in fact a very large part of everyone's normal mental processes.[1]

USE OF IMAGERY BY CONDUCTORS AND TEACHERS

Many conductors, coaches, and teachers of performance routinely make use of images to get their interpretive ideas across. I remember Jean Morel[2] suggesting at a conductors' institute: "more *staccato*!" and, after hearing the execution, bursting out, "no, no! Not like the thrust of a spear! It must be like a pinprick!" The result was immediate and magical. The admonition "more *staccato*!" obviously did not elicit the desired response. Perhaps Mr. Morel might also have asked for more *piano*; but it was the image of a pinprick which instantly produced the proper effect, i.e., the exact degree and combination of "short" and "soft."[3]

---

[1] It will be useful to define the terms "image," "imagination," and "imagery." The following is quoted from the *Oxford Universal Dictionary* (additional meanings which don't apply in this context have been disregarded):

Image:	a mental representation of something; a mental picture or an impression; an idea or concept.
Imagination:	the action of imagining, or forming a mental concept of what is not actually present to the senses; the result of this, a mental image or idea; the power which the mind has of forming concepts beyond those derived from external objects.
Imagery:	mental images collectively or generally.

[2] Jean Morel (1903-1975), conductor and teacher at the Juilliard School of Music.

[3] It was Mr. Morel's *imagination* which made him think of "pinprick." His use of *imagery* enabled him to communicate to the conductor and the players the specific *image* which narrowed the range of options with respect to articulation and dynamics and made their response inevitable.

It should be noted here that knowing the difference between a pinprick and a spear thrust does not involve musical talent at all. As this little episode proves, however, images such as these can play a significant role in the interpretation of music, and their deliberate use provides an effective and reliable tool toward adding definition, refinement, and character to a performance.

For another example of a similar use of imagery one might mention the statement of Vladimir Ashkenazy[4] that he always thinks of orchestral sounds when he plays the piano. Obviously one can not do a *pizzicato* or produce the sound of an oboe on the piano; but merely imagining the effect of plucked strings or the tone color of the oboe—with its core of intensity—causes a pianist to extend the palette of piano sounds.

Any student will readily respond to the images put before him by his teacher, as will an orchestra player or chorus member to those conveyed by the conductor. But how can the aspiring performer learn to conjure up such images without the prompting of more experienced artists? Just as these artists before him, the student will discover that almost all musical ideas evoke images of some kind which in turn help in making a performance more meaningful and compelling. As a result he may well come to pay more and more attention to his own responses and associations as each piece of music unfolds.

IMAGERY AND PERFORMANCE

The tendency toward spontaneous associations of the kind described here will vary greatly from individual to individual; but almost any performer has the potential for some form of imagery which will enable him to make his performance more "imaginative," in other words, more evocative, vital, and compelling.

It must be pointed out that the term "image" as we use it here has to be understood in the broadest sense and along a wide spectrum which ranges from abstract notions, barely perceptible feelings and sensations and subtle states of mind, all the way to vivid pictures of recognizable forms with clear contours and even well-defined colors.

As in all learning, the skills involved in the uses of imagery develop gradually and cumulatively. The process can be described in the following manner:

1.   Music evokes images, to begin with;

2.   The association music-image is usually involuntary and spontaneous;

3.   The spontaneous associations, which may initially be rather vague, can be turned into more viable images defining the character of a passage and thereby its interpretation;

---

[4]Quoted from *Beyond Frontiers*, by Jasper Parott and Vladimir Ashkenazy.

4.   When a musical passage evokes no immediate, tangible responses, the performer may well search for them consciously and deliberately. While examining a passage more closely, and particularly when assessing its character, mood, or emotional content, he will often be surprised at the clarity and even the multiplicity of the resulting associations.

WORDS IN A SCORE AND IMAGES

When words are part of a score, either in the form of a composer's instructions or comments, or of a text set to music, the images the words themselves evoke will greatly determine the details of interpretation. Rather than reacting haphazardly, the performer can make use of imagery in systematic fashion:

1.   To begin with, by taking note of all verbal hints composers put into their scores and by carefully determining their implications.

2.   There are innumerable works in which a title or a program[5] preceding the score will suggest an image or a whole series of images. *Träumerei, Feux d'artifice, Tod und Verklärung*, the latter with a poem supplying the program for the music to follow, provide stimulation and guidance and even specific hints for the performer's interpretation.

3.   Whenever words are set to music, the text itself will evoke a succession of images and determine the character and sequence of moods, which in turn will suggest many details of performance.

4.   In opera and musical theater the setting, the characters, action, and dialogue, will furnish a running series of clues for the subtler aspects of musical interpretation.

CONVENTIONAL MARKS OF EXPRESSION INADEQUATE

Many musical ideas seem to call for nuances which are too subtle to be sufficiently defined through notation or the conventional marks of expression. That is where the use of images can be most helpful, as the following examples will illustrate.

In programmatic pieces or musical episodes depicting rain—according to the title or some other hint—the dynamics and articulation marks generally are not explicit or varied enough. Rain comes in many gradations, from a barely perceptible noiseless drizzle to the deafening pounding of a cloudburst. Against the images of particular kinds of rain, however, the quality of articulation and the length and volume of the individual notes can readily be determined.

---

[5]"Non-musical idea . . . described in explanatory remarks or a preface" (*Harvard Dictionary of Music*) which provided the inspiration for "program" music.

For another illustration of the effect of an appropriate image on the musical execution let us consider a series of *forte* chords. Depending on the context, the performer might conjure up such images as handclapping (dry, sharp); sonic booms ("wham!"—longer, heavier); ear-splitting thunderclaps (very sharp, loud, overwhelming); or others yet. In each case the image, once selected, will determine duration and volume and invariably in ways that are considerably more specific than mere *staccato* dots or the indications *forte* or *fortissimo*.

These examples represent only two categories of—in these cases—concrete images. The scope of imagery, however, is unlimited. Any resourceful performer can expand the number of categories into a virtual vocabulary of imagery from which specific images can be culled to fit any particular passage.

The procedure is really quite simple and gradually comes to be applied as a matter of routine. In essence it involves the following steps:

1.   Playing or singing the passage in question;

2.   Determining its character or mood;

3.   Identifying an image or series of images which the musical passage evokes in the performer's mind;

4.   Modifying and refining the rendition of the passage in the light of these images.

There is always the danger that a performer may become enamored of particular images. Then he may carry the process so far that entire extra-musical fantasies are created which no longer have much to do with the musical ideas which gave rise to them. Obviously **the performer must at all times concentrate on the music itself and make sure that the images help him focus his attention on its essence rather than distracting him from it.**

ACTORS' METHODS USEFUL FOR MUSICIANS

It might be useful to draw attention to techniques employed by actors which have some bearing on the preparation for musical performance. When tackling a role, actors usually go through a rigorous process of study and analysis: "What is it exactly my character is saying, what is he trying to convey? What motivates him to say it, and say it in this way? Does he mean what he says or is he pretending?" The writer's choice of words and the formulation of each sentence suggest some underlying meaning which, once understood, will make the delivery more compelling and help the drama come alive.

The same kind of study and analysis applies where a text is set to music. Once the deeper meaning and all the implications of the text are grasped, the subtler interpretive inflections of the musical setting will easily fall into place. Even when there is no text, the same kind of probing will be productive; for it will help in clarifying the meaning of the music, its mood and emotional content, the significance of a particular turn of a phrase, etc.

The performer might also adopt another useful actor's device. When, for example, a scene requires an actor to commit some violent act outside the realm of his experience, he will obviously not indulge in violence himself just in order to learn how to make his enactment of the deed more convincing. Instead he will try to recall some past experience involving the kind of violent emotion which could conceivably lead to such an act. In other words, he will use substitute images enabling him to give a performance which has the ring of truth. The musician, too, can in the case of passages for which no ready interpretation offers itself find appropriate substitute images or some emotional or intellectual reference to fit the context.

"ABSOLUTE" MUSIC AND IMAGERY

What about the uses of imagery in the case of so-called absolute music which has no obvious literary or extra-musical references at all, e.g., works carrying only such designations as "symphony," "sonata," "string quartet," etc.? Most performers will find that here, too, images will involuntarily and quite spontaneously pass through their minds as the music unfolds, even though there are no extra-musical or programmatic references. Indeed, some of these may be images of concrete and even rather prosaic notions or objects, in spite of the abstract nature of the music.

IMAGERY AND PERFORMANCE

Actually our imagination functions most often on an intuitive and nonverbal plane, especially when it comes to music. This intuitive flux may involve feelings or sensations, and dreamlike and nearly subconscious associations. Sometimes these are visual, though they may be too vague to produce specific common images of recognizable objects. These undefined nonverbal associations are intensely personal and generally defy description and transference from one individual to another. Nevertheless, they are a very real and essential part of the interpretive process and effective tools in the preparation for any truly evocative and convincing performance.

To be sure, each performer has to discover within himself the kinds of associations to which he is predisposed and to learn to make use of his personal imagery in a way that clarifies and deepens his concepts and lends character and vitality to his performance.

Whether the images are concrete or abstract, whether they are tied to words, sensations or feelings, does not really matter. What does matter is that they translate readily into concepts of practical performance, i.e., tempo, dynamics, articulation, timbre, etc., or—to put it in the simplest terms, how fast—how slow?, how long—how short?, how loud—how soft?, etc.

The ultimate result of these various processes is that the performer acquires a heightened awareness and deeper perception of the essence and the spirit of the music he performs. If he is able and willing to abandon himself to that spirit, the music in turn becomes a living thing, so to speak, which imposes its will on him and possesses him, and through his performance transfixes and carries away his audience.

In the actual performance the process of "music evokes image" is reversed. The images which have become linked with their various musical ideas, in turn, become the tools the performer uses to trigger the corresponding interpretive responses. Imagery enters into all performances, whether as a conscious and deliberate device or not. Any performance involves a great many elements, most of them combined into a grand multiple reflex action through practice and conditioning. The essential point that needs to be understood is that after the innumerable details of preparation and training have been settled, all the elements come into play as a result of an intuitive process which involves an overriding all-encompassing series of images. Perhaps it is not inappropriate to compare the ultimate triggering action of the imaging process to pushing the button which activates a complex computer program.

This is how Yehudi Menuhin describes the phenomenon in his autobiography: "Intuition is born, I think, of many things happening at the same time . . . Our reason is geared to taking one problem on its own, analyzing it, and reaching a conclusion how we shall proceed. But when we are faced with ten different factors, all acting upon each other and among them creating some astronomical total of variables, reason is defeated and only intuition can cope."[6]

There is a near-parallel in the manner in which the Olympic diving champion Greg Louganis ascribes his almost unfailingly flawless performance to the use of imagery: he pictures each dive before his mind's eye, following it through in all its phases, but—at that point, immediately before the actual dive—without any preoccupation whatever with technical details.

There are innumerable stories of legendary musical giants whose performance invariably left an indelible impression. Their mere presence seemed to create a spell which no one present was able to escape, and they never failed to command instant attention, from the first note on. Among them were, to mention just a few, Liszt and Rachmaninoff, Mahler and Nikisch.[7]

When asked about the secret of their most gripping performances, many notable artists merely point to inspiration. But artistry and inspiration are abstractions which are, in one sense, beyond anyone's rational grasp; in another sense, however, they may be explained as the synthesis of the many subtle touches which together transform an indifferent performance into a vital and compelling one.

Not every performer may reach the exalted levels of supreme artists; but everyone can study and adopt some of the methods described here toward the realization of his full potential as an interpreter.

---

[6]Yehudi Menuhin, *Unfinished Journey*, p. 371.

[7]I shall never forget the performances conducted by Wilhelm Furtwängler which I was privileged to witness in my teens. From the moment he stepped on the podium he seemed in a trance, and the music-making was sheer magic, from beginning to end.

SELECTED BIBLIOGRAPHY

Bach, Carl Philipp Emanuel, *Essay on the True Art of Playing Keyboard Instruments*, transl. and ed. by William J. Mitchell. New York: W. W. Norton, 1949.

Barra, Donald, *The Dynamic Performance*. Englewood Cliffs, N. J.: Prentice-Hall, 1983.

Bartlett, John, *Familiar Quotations*, 14th ed., ed. by Emily Morison Beck. Boston: Little, Brown and Company, 1968.

Berry, Wallace, *Musical Structure and Performance*. New Haven: Yale University Press, 1989.

Blaukopf, Kurt, *Mahler*, transl. by Inge Goodwin. New York: Limelight Editions, 1985.

Butt, John, *Bach Interpretation, Articulation Marks in Primary Sources of J. S. Bach*. Cambridge: Cambridge University Press, 1990.

Cone, Edward T., *Musical Form and Performance*. New York: W. W. Norton, 1968.

Cooper, Grosvenor W. and Leonard B. Meyer, *The Rhythmic Structure of Music*. Chicago: University of Chicago Press, 1960.

Cooper, Paul, *Perspectives in Music Theory*, New York: Harper and Row, 1981.

Creston, Paul, *Principles of Rhythm*, New York: Franco Colombo, 1961.

Danuser, Hermann and Cristoph Keller, eds., *Aspekte der musikalischen Interpretation: Sava Savoff zum 70. Gerburtstag*. Hamburg: Karl Dieter Wagner Verlag, 1980.

Del Mar, Norman, *Conducting Beethoven*, Vol. I., The Symphonies. Oxford: Clarendon Press, 1992.

Donington, Robert, *The Interpretation of Early Music*, London: Faber and Faber, 1963.

Encyclopædia Britannica, 14th ed. Chicago: Encyclopedia Britannica, 1949.

Ericksen, Robert, *The Structure of Music*, 2nd ed. New York: The Noonday Press, 1959.

Furtwängler, Wilhelm, *Concerning Music*, transl. by L. J. Lawrence. London: Boosey and Hawkes, 1953.

Gallway, W. Timothy, *The Inner Game of Tennis*. New York: Random House, 1974.

Green, Barry, *The Inner Game of Music*. Garden City, N. Y.: Anchor Press/Doubleday 1986.

Harvard Dictionary of Music, ed. by Willi Apel, 2nd ed. Cambridge: Harvard University Press, 1986.

Keller, Hermann, *Phrasing and Articulation*, transl. by Leigh Gerdine. New York: W. W. Norton, 1973.

Kenyon, Nicholas, ed., *Authenticity and Early Music*. New York: 1988.

Kerman, Joseph, *Listen*, 3rd ed. New York: Worth, 1980.

Korn, Richard, *Orchestral Accents*. New York: Farrar, Straus, and Cudahy, 1956.

Leinsdorf, Erich, *The Composer's Advocate*. New Haven: Yale University Press, 1981.

Matthay, Tobias, *Musical Interpretation*, 5th ed. Boston: The Boston Music Company, 1913.

Menuhin, Yehudi, *Unfinished Journey*. New York: Alfred A. Knopf, 1977.

The New Grove Dictionary of Music and Musicians, 6th ed. London: Macmillan, 1980.

Neumann, Frederick, *Ornamentation in Baroque and Post-Baroque Music*. Princeton, N. J.: Princeton University Press, 1978.

The Oxford Universal Dictionary, rev. ed. Oxford: Clarendon Press, 1955.

Parrott, Jasper, with Vladimir Ashkenazy, *Beyond Frontiers*. New York: Atheneum, 1985.

Prausnitz, Frederik, *Score and Podium*. New York: W. W. Norton, 1983.

Quantz, Johann Joachim, *On Playing the Flute*, transl. by E. R. Reilly, 2nd ed. Translation of *Versuch einer Anweisung die Flöte traversiere zu spielen* (Berlin, 1752) New York: Schirmer Books, 1975.

Riemann, Hugo, *Handbuch der Phrasierung*, 8th ed. Berlin: Max Hesse, 1912.

Rosenblum, Sandra P., *Performance Practices in Classic Piano Music: Their Principles and Applications*. Bloomington: Indiana University Press, 1988.

Sachs, Curt, *Rhythm and Tempo*. New York: W. W. Norton, 1953.

SELECTED BIBLIOGRAPHY

Singher, Martial, *An Interpretive Guide to Operatic Arias*. University Park: Pennsylvania State University Press, 1983.

Stanton, Royal, *Steps in Singing for Voice Classes*. 3rd ed. Belmont, Calif.: Wadsworth Publishing Company, 1983.

Stein, Erwin, *Form and Performance*. New York: Alfred A. Knopf, 1962.

Stevens, Wallace, "Sunday Morning," IV, in *Six American Poets*, ed. Joel Connaroe. New York: Random House, 1991.

Swarowsky, Hans, *Wahrung der Gestalt*, ed. by Manfred Huss. Vienna: Universal Edition, 1979.

Thurmond, James M., *Note Grouping: A Method for Achieving Expression and Style in Musical Performance*. Ft. Lauderdale, Fla.: Meredith Music, 1982.

Toch, Ernst, *The Shaping Forces of Music*. New York: Criterion Music Corporation, 1948.

Türk, Daniel Gottlob, *Klavierschule*, 1789, facs. reprint. Basel: Bärenreiter, 1962.

Weisberg, Arthur, *Performing Twentieth Century Music: A Handbook for Conductors and Instrumentalists*. New Haven: Yale University Press, 1993.

Wolff, Konrad, *The Teaching of Artur Schnabel*. London: Faber and Faber, 1972.

INDEX

ABOUT THE AUTHOR

Hans Lampl began musical studies (piano, violin, viola, and theory) in his native Vienna. Having moved to the United States, he served during World War II with a U. S. infantry band as sousaphone player and occasional band leader. In due course, he obtained his Bachelor of Music and Master of Music (piano) degrees and Doctor of Musical Arts (conducting) from the University of Southern California. He taught at the University of Southern California, Michigan State University, and California State University, Long Beach, mostly performance-related courses (piano, accompanying, diction, conducting, choir, orchestra, and opera workshop). For twenty-two years, he was also conductor and music director of Southern California orchestras (Compton Civic Symphony, ten seasons and Rio Hondo Symphony, twelve seasons). He is a frequent guest conductor, clinician, adjudicator, and lecturer.